1586

BOUNDARIES

BOUNDARIES

WHERE YOU END AND I BEGIN

Anne Katherine, MA

PARKSIDE Publishing Corporation
205 West Touhy Avenue
Park Ridge, Illinois 60068

Katherine, Anne
  Boundaries

ISBN 0-942421-31-0

Printed in the United States of America

10 9 8 7 6 5 4 3 2

To Sherry

*I joyfully thank my clients, those special people who gave
me permission to tell their stories so that others who hurt
might heal.*

CONTENTS

"Good fences make good neighbors"

—Robert Frost

CHAPTER ONE

THE WALL BETWEEN

Laura's Story

I was born a month premature. In those days, preemies were put in an incubator and left alone. In my imagination, armed with what I've gleaned from years of therapy, I can return to those first days. What I see first looks like a tunnel with a clear roof. I am looking up through the incubator. A bright light shines all the time. The walls beyond are plain and white. I feel cut off from everyone and don't know who I belong to. The only time I am touched is to be cleaned.

Recently, I asked my mother how much she held me those weeks we were still in the hospital after my birth.

"Why, I held you all the time!" she said.

"How much?" I insisted. All the time was not my memory.

"Why, whenever they'd let me."

"How often was that?" I persisted.

"I held you every time they brought you to me to be fed," she said. "Twenty minutes, three times a day."

An hour a day my first three weeks of life. My baby self knew that wasn't nearly enough.

That touch deprivation continued. When I was six months old my father left my mother, so she left me with my grandparents and took off. My grandparents were not the most demonstrative people in the world. Maybe I saw them kiss each other once in all the years I lived with them. Me, they never touched.

When I was ten my mother remarried and decided she wanted me back. The second night I was in their house—my mother worked nights—my stepfather came into my room and got into bed with me.

After never being touched or held, I felt hands on my body. His touch made me feel sick inside. Something told me this wasn't right but nothing had ever told me that my feelings mattered or that I had a choice about anything. So I put up with it.

I remember the first time a boy touched me. I was thirteen, he was sixteen. We were at a teen dance and all I could think about was that I finally had a boyfriend. He danced with me and kept his arm around me all night. Was I jubilant? Was I thrilled? No, I was terrified. The only kind of touch I'd ever known disgusted me.

This was a nice boy who was completely proper and respectful, but when he put his arm across my shoulders I felt sick. My heart was beating so loudly from fear I could hear its pounding cadence in my ears. Far from enjoying my first healthy experience with a boy, my heart beat like that far into the night, hours after I was home alone. I avoided his calls. I wouldn't see him again.

Beth's Story

My mother was over 40 when I was born. My father, older still, was a military man. He commanded the household and everything in it, especially me. From preschool on he had long, serious discussions with every one of my teachers. He watched what I ate, directed my play, and as I got older interviewed my friends. It was he who taught me the neat way to dress, the proper way to sit and stand, and the meaning of duty, obedience, and loyalty.

When I had my first period, however, we were both shocked. Until then I had been perfect—straight As, conducting myself with proper military bearing. I was the son he'd never had. But becoming a woman interrupted my perfection. He didn't have to tell me but I knew I'd failed him in a big way. So I stopped eating. Eventually I stopped looking like a woman and my period stopped. My mother was concerned but my father wasn't. And since she didn't have a lot of say in our house nothing happened. Eventually, however, I was so thin and had so much trouble concentrating that my mother insisted I see a doctor. The doctor put me in the hospital immediately.

My father didn't want me away from him, but my therapists said I was anorexic and needed treatment. They forced me to eat. When my therapy group upset me, I called my father and he told me not to listen to them. He called my counselor and argued with her that nothing was wrong with me. The more he talked to me, the more I realized that it was ridiculous for me to be in the hospital. Those people didn't know what they were talking about. I was just fine. Besides, I missed him. He needed me. Finally my father came to get me. He didn't even care that insurance would no longer cover the costs because I'd left against medical advice. He wanted me with him that much.

Boundaries—What Are They?

Therapists and recovering people toss the word around easily. But what do they mean? Why have these stories been included? Do they say something about boundaries? Maybe not yet, but they will.

In this chapter we'll look at the big picture, boundaries from an eagle's point of view. Later we'll close in on the details. We'll swoop down on specific aspects of boundaries so that you'll recognize both the forest and the trees.

Exercises pepper the chapters. Enjoy them. Most are brief. Some involve other people. All let your body and heart in on the knowledge you're collecting with your mind—in learning what boundaries are all about.

An Amoeba Is Not a Tulip

So what is a boundary? A boundary is a limit or edge that defines you as separate from others.

Your skin is a boundary. Everything within your skin is the physical you.

Each living organism is separated from every other living organism by a physical barrier. Amoebae, orange trees, frogs, leopards, bacteria, tulips, turtles, salmon—all have physical limits that delineate them as unique from other organisms. This limit can be breached by injury or other organisms. If the breach is severe enough or if the invading organism is toxic or hostile, the host organism can die. An intact physical boundary preserves life.

Even an organism's physical components have boundaries. Your nerves are covered with a sheath or membrane. Your bones are distinct from your muscles. The physical world abounds with boundaries. Were it not so, when we sat down, we'd pass right through the chair (and the chair through us) and be sprawled on the floor. Except then we'd pass through the floor, too. And then the earth? Where would we stop?

We Are Surrounded by an Invisible Circle

Our skin marks the limit of our physical selves, but we have another boundary that extends beyond our skin. We become aware of this when someone stands too close. It's as if we are surrounded by an invisible circle, a comfort zone. This zone is fluid. A lover, say, can stand closer than most friends, and a friend can stand closer than a stranger. With someone who is hostile we might need a great deal of distance.

We have other boundaries as well—emotional, spiritual, sexual, and relational. You have a limit to what is safe and appropriate. You have a border that separates you from others. Within this border is your *youness*, that which makes you an individual different and separate from others.

What is an emotional boundary? We have a set of feelings and reactions that are distinctly ours. We respond to the world uniquely based on our individual perceptions, our special histories, our values, goals, and concerns. We can find people who react similarly, but no one reacts precisely as we do.

My Size Is None of Your Business

When it comes to how others treat us emotionally, we have limits on what is safe and appropriate. I came out of a store in downtown Seattle and a stranger started screaming at me about a religious matter. I turned and walked away. I do not have to accept screaming from anyone. I will accept appropriate anger from my friends and loved ones, but even then, I determine how close I'm willing to be to an angry person.

When I was younger, my landlady routinely commented about my weight. "You're getting bigger, ain't cha."

I let her say those things to me because I didn't know any better. Now I know that no one has a right to comment on my body. If that happened today, I'd tell her, "My size is none of your business and I want you to keep those thoughts to yourself." If she persisted, I'd also persist. I might never again deal with her in person. I might even move, whatever it would take to protect my emotional boundaries.

I used to let my clients say anything they wanted to me. If their need to be angry is that urgent, I thought, let them learn anger with me. Now I sacrifice myself for no one. If a client says something that hurts, I set a limit. Clients can be angry with me, and they can tell me so, but meanness and hostility advance neither the relationship nor the individual. If I let someone abuse me verbally, I have done neither one of us a favor.

The same is true for you. When you let someone abuse you or hurt you verbally, the other person is not advanced. Protecting yourself sets a necessary limit for both of you. That limit advances the relationship.

We have spiritual boundaries. You are the only one who knows the right spiritual path for yourself. If someone tries to tell you he knows the only way you can believe, he's out of line. "You must work out your own salvation with fear and trembling." (Philippians 2:12, New English Bible) We can be assisted but not forced. Our spiritual development comes from our inner selves.

We have sexual boundaries, limits on what is safe and appropriate sexual behavior from others. We have a choice about who we interact with sexually and the extent of that interaction.

We have relational boundaries. The roles we play define the limits of appropriate interaction with others.

In later chapters, we'll explore and further define these kinds of boundaries. But why so much talk about boundaries? Why are they so important?

Boundaries bring order to our lives. As we learn to strengthen our boundaries, we gain a clearer sense of ourselves and our relationship to others. Boundaries empower us to determine how we'll be treated by others. With good boundaries, we can have the wonderful assurance that comes from knowing we can and will protect ourselves from the ignorance, meanness, or thoughtlessness of others.

Touching Tells Us Where We Begin and End

How do we develop boundaries? Boundaries begin to form in infancy. In a healthy family a child is helped to individuate, to develop a self-concept separate and unique from the other family members.

Early on, Laura and Beth both received consistent family messages about boundaries. Beth had a father who wouldn't let her individuate; he didn't or couldn't let her develop separately, with values and an outlook different from his own. She therefore had no boundary with her father. By insisting that she think and be a certain way he prevented her from developing emotional boundaries. He denied her femaleness which catapulted her into anorexia, and thus violated her physical boundaries. He sabotaged treatment, preventing her from receiving the nutrition her body needed, and ultimately was prepared to risk her life rather than let her develop an identity separate from his. Beth's father was *enmeshed* with her.

Laura, on the other hand, was exposed to boundaries set far too distant for an infant and growing child. After being a part of our mother's body, we are thrust into the world as a separate entity. We depend on touch for our first sense of ourselves. Touching tells us where we are, where we end. Cuddling and holding tells us where we belong and that we do belong somewhere with someone.

A wonderful new type of birthing is spreading. After birth, which occurs in warm water, a massage therapist gently helps the baby unfold from the crumpled position he or she's held for so long. The therapist carefully stretches the small cramped limbs and lightly massages the tiny muscles. "Welcome, Baby. This is you. We will help you know yourself. We are with you. We know your needs."

From the earliest days of her life Laura was seriously deprived of touch. In contrast to the enmeshment Beth experienced, Laura lived in a family that set boundaries so far away from themselves that each person moved in a separate circle, so disconnected that Laura seemed to be growing up all by herself. By the time she was ten, she'd felt alone for so long that it didn't occur to her to ask for help in handling her stepfather's incestuous behavior. She expected to handle it alone.

Like Beth, Laura had no sense of her own boundaries. The lack of healthy physical and emotional contact from her family deprived her of developing a sense of her limits and how to protect them.

Put Up with My Behavior and You'll Be Okay

Incest is a grave violation of physical, emotional, and sexual boundaries. Laura's feelings told her that she didn't like what her stepfather was doing. But feelings had never been talked about or tended to in her family. Each person, within his or her separate circle, was expected to put up with hardship and do his duty regardless of feelings.

Her stepfather was asking her to act in spite of her feelings. When we are forced to act against our internal messages, feelings become increasingly more difficult to bear. Slowly, feelings themselves change from a friend to a betrayer that only brings pain. (This takes place over the years.) This effect of incest is one of the most serious damages of all, to cause these harmful splits within a person, splits that result from having learned to act contrary to feelings.

If you grew up in a dysfunctional family, you probably had little help with boundary development. You may have grown up without any clear sense of your own boundaries. In fact, you may have been taught to let others run over your boundaries.

We learn about our boundaries by the way we are treated as children. Then we teach others where our boundaries are by the way we let them treat us. Most people will respect our boundaries if we indicate where they are. With some people, however, we must actively defend them.

Boundaries Require Maintenance

Your skin is an obvious example of your physical boundary. Your emotional and relational boundaries may be less obvious, but they are just as important.

If the barrier of your skin is breached by a scratch, you become vulnerable to infection. If your emotional or relational boundaries are breached, you also become vulnerable to harm. When these invisible boundaries are trespassed by the thoughtless or intrusive actions of others, it is called a boundary violation.

Like any fence, boundaries require maintenance. Some people are like ivy. They keep trying to crawl over or through our boundaries. It's tiresome, but if we let these people stay in our lives, we must keep pruning them and throwing the behavior weeds out of our yards.

What are boundaries like? Are they rigid or stiff? If I have a boundary that limits hostile comments from others, am I also walling out compliments?

Boundaries come in assorted shapes and sizes. They can be rigid like a brick wall or as flexible as a plastic bag, as impenetrable as a lead shield or as permeable as a chain-link fence. Some boundaries are transparent, others are opaque. Boundaries can be so far out that people can hardly get within yelling distance. Or they can be so close that, in the words of Groucho Marx, "If I were any closer, I'd be in back of you." Chapter Six describes different boundaries in more detail.

What is seen as a healthy boundary in one country or culture may be misunderstood or feared in another culture. Actions interpreted as boundary violations by white people in the United States may be common customs in Native American circles. U.S. citizens, with their easy familiarity, may unwittingly violate boundaries in other more formal countries by practices common within our own borders.

In a recent training session of Goodwill Games volunteers, this heterogeneous group of about 2000 Americans of varied ages and backgrounds was asked to rank a series of values. With few exceptions, honesty, growth, and independence were rated as the top three. At the bottom of the list of 20 values were formality, obedience, and tradition. Many cultures of the world would have reversed the order, placing tradition and formality at the top and honesty and independence at the bottom.

Such basic differences can create a clash of boundaries. An open-faced American rushing in with extended hand and first names violates a culture prizing formal ritual in initial contacts with strangers. We may view the strong Soviet value of community loyalty as a lack of individual independence. Soviets may find our directness rude and boastful. Boundaries, to some extent then, are influenced by the values of the culture in which we live. When we interact with other cultures, it's important to be sensitive to these differences and to remember that each side may unwittingly cross a boundary not from malice but from ignorance.

I Am Not You

Our emotional health is related to the health of our boundaries. When we grow up in a dysfunctional family, learning how to use boundaries is one of the most uncomfortable set of clothes to try on. It threatens our former understanding of survival itself and in that way goes against our very grain. But with time the wardrobe changes. We come to see ourselves as clearly separate from others, yet not too distant, and if our boundaries are intact we have a sense of well-being. Intact, clear boundaries feel good. Healthy boundaries are flexible enough that we can choose what to let in and what to keep out. We can determine to exclude meanness and hostility and let in affection, kindness, and positive regard.

Where are your boundaries? Do you know? Do you have a sense of your edges, your uniqueness? Are you comfortable within your limits?

Picture Your Boundary

Exercise 1.1

Equipment: twine or string at least 25 feet long

1. In the middle of a room with lots of space, put the twine on the floor so that it makes a circle. Stand in the middle of the circle. Imagine that everything outside the circle is not you. Imagine that everything within the circle is you.

2. Think about what fills up your circle. What do you care about? What do you believe? What do you hate? What do you love? Who are you? What is attractive to you? What repels you? What do you value? What do you think about? What are you really like?

3. A million things make you distinct from everyone else. The more you know about these things, the firmer your self-concept.

   Option a. Write the answers to these questions.

   Option b. Discuss these questions and their answers with a friend.

Exercise 1.2

Equipment: magazines, large paper grocery bag, tape or glue

1. From the magazines, cut or tear pictures or words that describe the external you, the you that is presented to the world.

2. Paste or tape the pictures or words on the outside of the bag.

3. Inside the bag put the words or pictures that describe your inside self.

4. After you're done, compare the words and pictures inside the bag with those outside the bag. Have you described two different people?

5. Discuss your discoveries with a friend.

Boundaries Quiz

Exercise 1.3 (Optional) Just for fun, see how much you've learned about boundaries, either here or through living.

I. Multiple Choice. Choose the correct answer.

    A. The word boundary, as used today by therapists and recovering people, refers to one's
      1. Physical and sexual limits
      2. Emotional and spiritual limits

      3. Relational limits
      4. All of the above

  B. The phrase boundary violation indicates
      1. That one's limits have been breached
      2. That one has expanded his or her frontiers
      3. A minor infringement of one's defenses
      4. None of the above

  C. A boundary violation causes
      1. No particular consequence
      2. An emotional shock wave
      3. No harm to a really strong relationship
      4. A problem only to the victim of the violation

  D. Boundaries are
      1. Usually flexible
      2. Usually rigid
      3. Impossible to change
      4. Different for different people

II. Mark the incidents that are boundary violations.
  A. Grandpa takes little Jim fishing.
  B. Esther tells Betty a secret Mary told her.
  C. Your therapist invites you to go for coffee.
  D. Your boss wants to know details of your personal life.
  E. Your boss cries on your shoulder.
  F. Your therapist accepts your invitation to go for coffee.
  G. Mom tells little Debby about her problems with Dad.
  H. Your boss asks if you'd like a hug.
  I. Your new neighbor pats you on the bottom as he turns away.
  J. Your mother makes a comment about you being overweight.

Answers. I. A. 4.; B. 1.; C. 2.; D. 4. II. Letters A and H are the
only incidents that aren't boundary violations.

CHAPTER TWO

VISIBLE AND INVISIBLE BOUNDARIES

Laura's Story

I remember this brief incident that occurred when I was fifteen. I was walking downtown and a strange man started walking beside me. He was much older than me, dirty looking, and he began talking to me using gestures that involved touching my arm, shoulder, head, and waist.

I had no idea how to handle the situation. I'd been taught to be courteous to everyone. It never occurred to me that I could limit how a person touched me or that I could stop a person from touching me. I had no idea how to stand up for myself or even that standing up for myself was an option.

The farther we walked, the more bold he got. At one point he was touching my breasts and I was still fighting to be nice to him, to listen to him politely. But I finally got so uncomfortable that I told him I had to be somewhere. I ran into a department store. It never occurred to me to mention this incident to my mother.

One of my high school teachers was Mr. Elliot. Every day for four years I sat in his classroom. Mr. Elliot had a notorious reputation among the students. It was well known that he touched girls if they stood too close to him.

Once when one of my classmates went up to his desk to ask him a question, he ran his hand up and down her leg the whole time they were talking. Another time I was standing at his desk with a friend of mine and he kept staring at her breasts. Then he turned his head and winked at me. Was this supposed to be a joke? Was I supposed to find it funny?

I didn't want him to touch me, so I kept well away from him if I had to go up to his desk. He looked me over just the same. This man was a friend of my parents and grandparents, but I was not exempt.

He touched and looked at so many girls that upperclassmen warned underclassmen about him when they entered high school. Looking back, it boggles my mind that so many girls had this man's number and it wasn't leaked to a parent or two. How could he act this way for decades and the administration not catch on and stop him?

Another scene comes to me from movies I saw when I was a kid. A woman would be angry with a man, maybe she would turn her back on him or walk away from him. Then he would come after her, catch her, and kiss her against her will. All this time she is struggling but suddenly she surrenders and throws her arms around him.

As I was growing up, I was exposed to plenty of stuff that said if a man wanted to touch you, you had to go along with it. Nothing taught me I could say no.

When I was a sophomore in college, I went on a date with a senior. We went to a drive-in. During the movie he kept taking swigs from a bottle—I think it was whiskey—and he kept asking me if I wanted some. All I could think about was my stepfather's drinking. I couldn't even take a sip.

He started touching me. It felt awful but I didn't know I had a choice. So I put up with it. At least my dorm had a curfew. That's all I could think about. When he took me back, we sat in his truck till right before the dorm closed. I was watching the building, he was pushing up against me and finally the dorm lights blinked the five-minute warning. I didn't go out on a date for two years after that.

The only way I knew how to deal with men was to stay away from them. I didn't know people talked about these things, so I never told anyone. I never had a class or a teacher—nobody ever told me that women had a right to limit how their bodies were touched or how this was done.

When I was a senior, I did some traveling. I met this man in Rome. He was kind to me. One day he took me on a tour and then out to dinner. He said he wanted me to meet his cousin, who was staying with him, but when we got to his apartment the only cousin I saw was in a picture beside his bed.

I had no idea where in Rome I was and my Italian was pretty rudimentary, but I ran out of his apartment and down the stairs. He came running after me and said he would take me back to my hotel. I said o.k.

On the way back, he stopped the car and pressed himself against me. I put up with it. Why I could walk out of his apartment and not his car, I don't know. Perhaps I was more frightened in his apartment, perhaps I felt that since we were on the way to my hotel, it was almost over and I could take it. At any rate, I put up with his pressing until he'd gotten what he wanted. I considered it not so bad because it wasn't skin to skin and he was able to climax without penetrating me or requiring me to touch him. I thought about something else until he was done. The part I hated was the look I got from the hotel concierge as I came through the doors at 3:30 in the morning. He made me feel dirty. I wanted to tell him I was innocent.

Georgia's Story

When I think about my early childhood, I don't have visual memories that unreel like videotape. It's more like my body has recorded my experiences, and when I focus on a certain age my body offers these awarenesses connected with that time.

I have strong awarenesses connected with my older brother. I sense I was an infant when he began molesting me. He would have been eight at the time. He must have told me he would kill me if I told because now, 30 years later, I still feel that I'm going to die when I talk about this.

I can't be sure what he actually did. That's part of what's so maddening about it. I know something awful happened, yet if somebody asked me what, I couldn't pin down enough details to convince somebody I was telling the truth. Sometimes it seems so vague I think I must be making it up.

He must have had his bare body on mine. He must have had an erection and a climax, because I had too much sexual knowledge too young. He must have poked his fingers into me. I feel such a deep sense of shame around certain parts of my body. This went on for many years, I feel sure.

When I finally told my parents about it in therapy they said, "Why didn't you tell us?"

I felt like screaming when they said that. I felt hopeless and pinned down. I wanted to yell at them, "Just when was I going to tell you? While you were beating me, Mom? Was that the opportune time to tell you? Or perhaps during one of your hysterical rages?"

I was so defeated by that question, I couldn't tell them what it was like for me. Why didn't they know what it was like for me in that house?

I was overwhelmed all the time when I was a kid with all I had to do. I was taking care of the little kids and trying to make sense out of a senseless household. The house was always so filthy. I was ten

years old and trying to keep up with it somehow—trying to clean
the house, trying to keep the grass mowed, trying to take care of
my sisters.

I kept hoping she'd notice. I kept hoping she'd notice that my
job was too big. I hoped she'd notice what he was doing to me. I
wanted her to know. I would try to talk to her, to test her to see if
it was safe yet to tell her what he was doing to me. Every time, her
response showed me it wasn't safe yet.

I was constantly defending myself against *her*. I wanted to say in
that therapy session, "What did you ever do to lead me to believe
you could handle that situation with my brother? You just might
have beaten me because of it."

"Or Dad, when was I gonna tell you? You were working fourteen
hours a day. You were never home. You had no idea what your wife
was doing while you were gone. Did you work so hard to get away
from her? If you didn't want to be with her, how did you justify
leaving six defenseless kids with her?

"Our home was so safe and peaceful, we were so encouraged to
talk about what we were going through, I'm shocked it slipped my
mind that Bobby was crawling on top of me and poking himself into
me." That's what I wanted to say.

Donna's Story

I must have been three or four when my dad started fondling me.
I remember the before and after but I don't remember the middle. I
remember he was taking me to the river in his truck. He was going
to show me the boats on the river. Then I remember being home
and that he was changing my underpants. My mom came into the
bedroom and asked what was going on and he said I had an accident
and so we never got to the river because he had to bring me home to
change clothes.

I get confused when I try to remember what happened when. My
parents separated and then got back together. Two of my cousins
said Dad had touched them, so we never did anything with my aunt
and uncle and cousins again. My dad was accused of molesting a
girl in the neighborhood and he got off. How come my mother
never considered what might be happening to me?

He started in on me again when I was nine. I think I was twelve
when I told my mother. She talked to him and told me he promised
never to do it again. And she believed him. I wanted to, but I soon
found out he would do it again.

Yet, after all, I really loved my father. My mother never had the time of day for me. When she wasn't working, which wasn't much —she was a corporate executive—all she wanted to deal with was her hair and her clothes and her makeup. And then she was too tired for anything else. She didn't want me to bother her.

A Mark Is Left
The skin—it's a physical boundary, a barrier that keeps the body intact. A cut or scratch is not the only type of physical harm that can cause damage. The wrong person's hand on the body for the wrong reason can also harm.

It doesn't cause a scratch, you might argue. The person's not *really* harmed. No mark is left.

I would disagree with you. A mark *is* left. Any physical violation is also a violation of a person's emotional boundaries.

Later in the chapter on boundary violations, we'll discuss various types of harm. For now, however, we'll consider two types of boundaries and two categories of violations.

We Have Reverse and Forward Gears
The two main types of boundaries are physical and emotional. Our physical limits are marked by our skin; our emotional limits, by age, roles, our relationships with those around us, our requirements for safety, and our choices about how we want to be treated.

I set my physical boundary by choosing who can touch me and how and where I am touched. I decide how close I'll let people come to me. Because I have a reverse gear as well as a forward I can back away from someone who invades my personal zone.

I set my emotional boundary by choosing how I'll let people treat me. One way I do this is by setting limits on what people can say to me. Healthy, safe expressions of anger or even rage by people I'm close to are very acceptable. Inappropriate anger from an inappropriate person is not. A stranger on a bus will not get to vent his anger with me. I'll change seats or get help from the driver if necessary.

I determine the range of personal comments I'll accept from others. One of my aunts, for example, comments freely about the bodies of those with her. My cousin and I were at dinner with her when a stranger (to us) came by the table. "We're eating," said my aunt, "even though none of us needs to." I had given this aunt a lot of slack because I love her very much. But in thinking about it later, I realized I'd felt bad when she said it and that I didn't want her including me when she makes those comments.

Sometimes we think that if we've let someone do something once, we have to let him or her do it again. On the contrary, we can change our minds, discover that we didn't like something someone said, and set new standards of behavior.

I stop sexual comments and innuendos from men I work with and men I meet casually. I decide how much personal information I'll reveal to others. I evaluate how others treat what I do reveal, which helps me decide whether to trust them with any more. And when it comes to personal questions I decide which ones I'm willing to answer.

I told something very personal to an aunt I love. She in turned passed it along in a letter (inaccurately) to relatives I don't trust. In the future I'll be more careful about what I tell her.

To another relative I opened my heart only to find out indirectly that she thought I was playing games with her. I hadn't detected that at all in our communications. So since she could not express her feelings directly—since in fact how she appeared directly contradicted what she was thinking—I realized I could never know her real reactions to me. This discovery also showed me that she changes the meaning of what I tell her. So since I cannot control how she'll think or trust that she'll discuss her reactions with me— but I can be certain that she'll distort what I tell her and pass on the distortions—I can't have a relationship with her.

Setting emotional boundaries includes deciding what relationships I'll foster and continue and what people I'll back away from because I can't trust them.

Prime Violations

Violations come in two main categories: violations of intrusion and violations of distance. At the beginning of this chapter, Laura, Georgia, and Donna described violations of physical intrusion. In the previous chapter, Beth described emotional intrusion and Laura described physical and emotional violations of distance.

Intrusion violations: "Have you ever had an abortion?" Violations of intrusion occur when a physical or emotional boundary is breached. Incest is a violation of intrusion. Other violations of intrusion include inappropriate personal questions, inappropriate touching, and attempting to control how another thinks, believes, or feels.

Appropriate closeness is defined by context, by the type of relationship. The type of intimacy sought between husband and wife is out of place between parent and child. In Chapter Three, Context, we'll explore the limits determined by the type of relationship.

Georgia's brother placed his nude body on hers. He touched her sexually. Donna's father was sexual with her and other children. Laura's teacher, Mr. Elliot, touched the female students in his class. In each case, these men acted beyond the accepted bounds of the relationship. These were physical intrusion violations.

So, violations of physical intrusion include physical intimacy that goes beyond a level appropriate to the relationship.

A newcomer at my knitting club committed a violation of intrusion when she asked me if I'd ever had an abortion. I'd never seen her before. We had no basis on which to speak of something so personal. I don't have to bear the consequences of someone else's thoughtlessness or lack of awareness. If someone asks me a personal question that is inappropriate within the context of our relationship, I don't have to answer it.

As it happens, I haven't had an abortion. I could have said "No," but I didn't want to give her the message that I thought the question was all right. I could have said "Why do you ask?" but the inappropriateness of the question made me reluctant to enter into conversation with her. What I did say was "I don't know you well enough to discuss something like that." She looked a little surprised, turned to someone else, and avoided me the rest of the meeting, which was fine with me. I don't need a friend who doesn't keep good boundaries.

Distance violations: "Adults also need to be touched." Violations of distance occur when intimacy is less than what is appropriate to the relationship, when someone from whom one has a right to expect closeness is excessively removed or cut off. If closeness is an appropriate part of a relationship and it does not occur, the relationship has too much distance. Again, context is the key that defines the violation.

It may be hard to see, but too much distance is harmful. Children need safe physical contact in order to define themselves. Nonsexual cuddling, hugging, holding, and touching are important for a child's emotional and physical development. Adults also need to be touched.

In *A Natural History of the Senses,* Diane Ackerman reports on experiments that show that the more babies are held, the higher their level of alertness and cognitive development, and that people of all ages can sicken in the absence of touching and being touched.[1]

At the beginning of this chapter, Laura related a series of incidents in which she was touched against her will. Why didn't she stop these men, walk out, just say no? (I have a new favorite T-shirt. It says, "What is it about the word NO that you don't understand?")

When we have good emotional boundaries we can protect our physical boundaries. But both physical and emotional boundary development are harmed by distance violations, not just intrusion violations.

Our ability to protect ourselves is related to the strength of our boundaries. If we haven't developed clear emotional boundaries, we are vulnerable to physical violation.

Laura, Georgia, and Donna received no safe physical affection as children. They were also neglected emotionally. Georgia's mother was angry and physically abusive; her father and Donna's mother were away from home and engrossed in work. Physical intrusion or incest is not intimacy. An incestor is hardly emotionally available to the victim. Thus one can be emotionally abandoned while being violated intrusively.

Since Laura's family didn't encourage talk about feelings, she didn't learn how to pull out internal information that she could use to take care of herself. Because she was emotionally abandoned and had no help bringing feelings into awareness she—and Georgia and Donna—never learned that feelings can be used to determine a course of action.

Our Feelings Are Rich in Information

When we yell, we know we yelled because we hear it (unless our hearing is impaired). Our ears give us immediate feedback that

---

[1] Diane Ackerman, "The Power of Touch," *Parade Magazine,* March 25, 1990, p. 5.

we've made a sound. We can then modify the sound to accurately convey what we mean.

Similarly, we need a reaction, feedback, when we're feeling something. When the feedback is accurate, our feeling unfolds and becomes clearer.

An echo bounces your words back to you. A warm response brings your feelings back to you. You get to know yourself better. This combination—of effective feedback and knowing yourself better—creates an emotional boundary. It fills in the circle of who you are and creates a space outside you of who you aren't.

Our feelings are rich in information about how we are reacting to the world. They tell us when something seems dangerous or threatening or safe. As children we are taught to write and speak a language and we are also taught how to handle feelings. We learn how to do this by watching others handle them and by the way our feelings are responded to.

"I'm scared!" says the five-year-old on the way to his first day of school.

"No, you're not. This is fun," says an uninformed dad.

"Mommy, I hurt myself!" The four-year-old comes running, cradling her scraped elbow.

"Oooh, let me see that," her mother responds warmly. "I'm sorry you got hurt." She picks her up, cuddles her, and carries her inside.

He's seven. His face is tight. His mouth is pinched. "I don't want to go to my Scout meeting."

Pretend you are seven and compare these two parental reactions:
- "Of course you do. The Scouts will teach you to be a man."
- "Come here, dear. You look scared. Tell me what happened."

Feelings Connect Us with Meaning

We learn emotional boundaries by the responses we get. When our feelings are met with disapproval, harshness, or stiff-upper-lip messages, we learn to push them down, to separate ourselves from our feelings, and to ignore the valuable information they have for us.

When feelings are met warmly, when we are encouraged to talk about them and helped to identify them, and when a parent correctly interprets our facial expression, our body language, and the feelings connected with it, our understanding of our inner selves grows. Learning about and connecting with feelings is essential for complete boundary development.

Look around you right now. Look at a tree outside the window or a picture on the wall. Let yourself connect with your feeling about that tree or that picture. Open to your responses. You discover the meaning it has for you through your feelings. If you have no feelings for it you'll have no connection to it. It will be as a blank wall to you.

I have a plastic shopping bag labeled in big red letters with the name of a local discount store. Every time I go to that store, I have to wait in line forever. I look at the bag and have a slightly negative feeling. The bag has meaning for me and I discover that meaning through my feelings.

I have another plastic bag labeled with the logo from Walt Disney World. I love that place, so when I re-use that bag, I have a positive feeling.

Our feelings are rich in meaning about the nature of our connections with others. When we are in contact with that, we can be guided by our inner selves, we can tell who we are, what is right for us. We can, therefore, know our emotional boundaries. And by knowing our emotional boundaries, we can tell when someone has breached them. Being connected with our inner selves gives us the strength to protect ourselves from violators. It's something we can do automatically. Like it says in the "Big Book," "if we are painstaking about this phase of our development, we will intuitively know how to handle situations which used to baffle us."[2]

Without a Mirror, We Can't See Ourselves

If, as we are growing, people are too emotionally distant, we grow as if in a vacuum. We don't have the necessary feedback, the echo, that helps us differentiate. Without a mirror, we can't see

---

[2] *Alcoholics Anonymous*, 3rd ed. (New York: Alcoholics Anonymous World Services, 1976), pp. 83–84.

ourselves. Children who've suffered from this type of abandonment adapt in several different ways.

Some become loners, unable to let anyone close. Having never connected with their own feelings, they have little ability to connect with others. Fred, whose story follows, is a good example of this.

Some fill themselves up with the identity of someone else. If our inner spaces are empty, we are vulnerable to filling them with someone else's agenda. Such a person can be like a chameleon, taking on the values and reactions of whomever they are with.

Sometimes a child is abandoned emotionally but taught to revere certain values. Laura was very much alone. Anyone in a void will cling to whatever's offered. What was offered she clutched. Her empty inner spaces were filled with pulsing messages to be courteous, especially to elders, to be helpful, to meet the needs of others, to be nice. And she was nice and courteous, even when a stranger was touching her breasts on a downtown street.

A child reared in an emotional void can be filled with fervent religious teachings, or a military ethic, or that work is holy and one's ultimate purpose is to make money and acquire things. A child in a void can fill up with this even if she is not actively taught. She need only observe and the vacuum will fill.

If one parent is emotionally distant and the other is enmeshed with the child, the void created by one parent is filled with the needs of the other. Usually, incest can repeatedly occur only if the parents are emotionally absent. An emotionally present parent would pick up on the injury in the child and intervene. Moreover, an incested child of an emotionally present parent would have enough responsive experiences from that parent to be able to communicate at least nonverbally that something's very wrong.

A parent may not know a child is being incested, but in most cases, by the emotional tone he or she sets, the parent can enable the incest to stop or to continue.

Fred's Story

I don't understand all this talk about feelings. They're irrelevant. I didn't get to be the head of a law firm at 42 by whining and wailing all the time. I usually don't talk about this but look at where I am. I've got a nice house in a secure suburb, a hot tub, central air, solid furniture. I never worry about my car breaking down. I make sure it's taken care of before a problem develops. I've been investing my money since I was ten. I don't have to worry about a thing. My money is secure and I am, too. I plan to retire when I'm 55 and I'll be able to live as well as I live now. Look at my life. There's the evidence. The way I live it works very well.

I can be proud of what I've done. I started working when I was nine. Got a paper route and in no time figured out that I could double my route and my profits with only half again as much work. Before I was twelve I was handling four routes.

Sure, I had fun when I was a kid. I took some time out toward the end of high school. I still worked, but my buddies and I, we had a great time.

I have to laugh. We'd play these pranks. Like one of our best was rearranging people's lawns. We started small, like exchanging the chairs on one porch for the chairs on the porch next door. Then we got more creative about it. Say Mr. Jones has a patio set, bird house, potted plants. In the middle of the night, we'd sneak these into the pickup, drive a few blocks to Mr. Smith's house, and exchange them for a kid's play set, toys, kiddy pool. Take the kid's stuff and arrange it in Mr. Jones' yard like it belonged there. Then we'd laugh all night thinking of the look on the faces of the Smiths and the Joneses when they came out in the morning.

Did we ever tell them where their stuff was? You mean like an anonymous call or a note? Naw, that was their problem. We never thought about it again, except to laugh about it when we'd be telling stories of our exploits. We never actually stole anything, well almost never, unless somebody had a plant or something one of our moms would like.

One of my dad's clients was a trial lawyer, very sharp, one of the best in the state. He always handled my cases when I was dragged in for something—DUI, reckless driving, you know. He always got me off.

My parents? They did well. My father was an investment banker. He worked hard all his life. He had a beautiful house, two stories, columns, French furniture, on five acres not far from the river. What a worker. He could fly back from a vacation and meet with a client that same night. I can't help but admire him. Of course, this kind of thing pissed off my mother in a quiet, cold way, but what a guy, barely off the plane from a pseudo-vacation and he's still got enough energy and wit to sell a client.

My mother? I don't think about her much. She made an art form out of being helpless. She looked to him for everything. We'd be out to dinner and her wine glass would get empty and she'd say, "Hugh! Hugh!" She might be sitting right next to the wine bottle, but he'd have to pour it for her.

I was pretty much raised by Alma Mae. She was our housekeeper the whole time I was growing up. Mother worked when I was real little and then later she spent a lot of time with the guy she had an affair with. She really didn't stay home much till later. After I was gone, I guess.

Reared in an Emotional Void

Fred demonstrates one consequence of having two emotionally distant parents. His father was a compulsive worker. His mother was also absent. Both showed signs of alcoholism. Fred is completely cut off from his feelings and, like his father, uses work and alcohol to keep it that way.

Because his feelings are blocked, he has poor access to insight or information about himself. He doesn't question the enormous energy he's invested in achieving security or that this need might be related to the excessive abandonment he experienced as a child. Reared in an emotional void, Fred inserted into it the only thing he knew—the persistent hard work he saw his father doing.

While growing up, Fred likely received no information about how to interact with others, how to have a relationship, or how to deduce warning signs from behavior. When he was a teenager, his family certainly didn't read the warnings in his repeated encounters with the law for drinking and driving. His father provided an expensive lawyer, but this was but another form of abandonment.

A child can have plenty of food, warm clothes, and a clean home yet be utterly emotionally abandoned. Without parental warmth and attention, emotional development withers.

So, to be healthy we must have clear physical and emotional boundaries. We must be able to defend ourselves physically by setting limits on how close we let people get, on who touches us, and on how we are touched. To do this, we need a definite sense of our emotional boundaries. When we enhance our sense of who we are and what we need, like, want, and feel, we strengthen our emotional boundaries.

Seeing Boundaries

Exercise 2.1

This exercise can raise your awareness of other people's boundaries. Use it as a time for information gathering and don't try to influence the interactions you see.

Physical Boundaries
1. Today, watch and listen carefully to the people around you. By what actions or words do they indicate and protect their physical boundaries—the distance others must keep for them to remain comfortable?
   a. If riding a bus, notice what people do when a stranger sits next to them.
   b. If walking downtown, notice the berth people give when passing others. How different is that distance from the people with whom they are walking?
   c. How close does the boss get to the workers?
   d. How close do the workers get to the boss?
   e. If someone speaks angrily, do the listeners move closer to or farther from the speaker?
   f. If someone speaks kindly, do the listeners change position?
   g. How close do your children come to you? How close do they get to your spouse?
   h. How close do you feel like getting to your children, to your spouse?
   i. As you stand talking to a person at work, move just a bit closer. What does the other person do? After a bit, or with a different person, step back a little. What does the other guy do?
   j. If you are fortunate enough to live in a place where people of other races or cultures live, observe how close they stand when they talk to a friend, a stranger.

Emotional Boundaries
2. Tomorrow observe how people keep and set emotional boundaries.
   a. Listen for remarks among people that are appropriate given their relationship and what they are doing.

b. Listen for remarks that are questionable or clearly inappropriate. How does the receiver handle the situation?

c. Watch your children. How do they protect their privacy from their siblings?

d. What does your spouse do to warn you off from private emotional territory?

e. How does your spouse communicate important needs and feelings? What happens when he or she feels or wants something different from what you feel or want?

CHAPTER THREE

CONTEXT

Context is Everything

Context, the type of relationship, defines appropriate closeness and distance in a relationship.

Certain relationships presume closeness. A marriage has the potential for great physical and emotional intimacy. The parent-child relationship offers a range of safe physical closeness and a range of emotional involvement. Best friends can share some physical closeness and a high degree of emotional intimacy.

Notice how the roles define the range of appropriate closeness. Sexual intimacy, desirable in a marriage or like partnership, is completely out of place between parents and children and in most friendships. Physical intimacy occurs along a continuum. At one end lives full sexual involvement (between committed partners); at the other, no contact of any kind (between strangers).

Just as context defines appropriate closeness, it also defines appropriate distance. In the context of marriage or commitment, appropriate emotional intimacy leads comfortably to physical intimacy. Little or no sexual or emotional affection between married or committed partners, however, is often a sign of problems in the relationship. It can mean too much emotional distance or violating closeness. (More about this later.)

Violations of distance happen when children don't get enough from their parents, when one spouse won't speak to the other, is emotionally cold, or is unwilling to discuss important matters, or when one friend refuses to work out a disagreement with another.

Thus context, the type of relationship, defines the appropriate range of closeness and distance. Between spouses there can be a range of closeness and distance, but there's a limit to what is healthy at each end of that range. Between parent and child another range exists. Exceeding the limits of appropriate distance and closeness causes a boundary violation.

Just Married

Marriage and other committed relationships theoretically offer the greatest opportunity and allowance for full physical and emotional intimacy. Marriage is possibly the most complicated of relationships. It has a profound impact and influence on the course of one's life. Yet frequently it is entered into with little thought and awareness, half-understood reasons, and poorly known influences.

Sometimes when I see a "Just Married" sign on a car, I imagine innocent lambs walking into a labyrinth or a four-year-old put into the cockpit of an engaged 747. I have to resist the impulse to run over to the car and push my card through the window. "Call in a couple of weeks—or tonight if necessary," I want to tell them. Since I have a few boundaries I don't act on my impulse. I'm almost compulsively appropriate.

Anyway, this subject deserves its own chapter and gets one in Chapter Six. So for now we'll just consider the appropriate range of closeness and distance in the context of an intimate partnership.

Us and Not-Us, You and Not-You

What is this range? The acceptable degree of intimacy and distance can vary in different marriages and within a single marriage from day to day.

Communication is the life-blood that keeps the partnership fluid and vital and clarifies each person's needs for intimacy and separateness.

Ideally, the marriage contains enough togetherness to preserve the boundary of us and not-us and enough separation to preserve each person's individuality.

In a healthy marriage or intimate partnership, each person is whole and intact. They choose to live together. They could still live if something happened to the other.

Marriages seem to have the best chance if the partners have a lot in common—shared interests, similar values, kindred goals, comparable backgrounds, roughly equal intelligence, and a somewhat parallel way of looking at things. Too much difference builds in too much distance.

On the other hand, each person is unique. This uniqueness contributes to the relationship and to the world. So it's critical for each person to have his and her own thoughts and feelings, and for each to take responsibility for his or her actions.

Enmeshment Is Not Intimacy

When one partner tries to influence the thinking of the other or wants the other to have exactly the same feelings, problems are inevitable. Falling in love feels exciting and involving, but the truth is, it's a fairly enmeshed stage of the relationship. Yes it is validating for someone to have thoughts and feelings identical to our own. It feels wonderful. Eventually, though, perceptions will differ. How this is handled is critical for the future of the relationship.

If Jack tries to overpower Jill's perceptions, thoughts, or feelings, if Jack insists that Jill's process is inferior or lacking, there's a problem.

Jill will need very good boundaries to withstand Jack's onslaught on her self-worth.

There's a big difference between enmeshment and intimacy. Enmeshment may feel like intimacy, but it is not. Intimacy comes from knowing each other very well, accepting shortcomings and differences, and loving each other anyway. Enmeshment is attempting to feel and think as if you were the same person. Since quite a bit of one's uniqueness is missed this way, neither person can really be known, a very different experience from intimacy.

Donna's Story

When I got married, the movies and magazines portrayed marriage as happily ever after. Women were like Donna Reed. They had little earning power but it didn't matter because this kind, wise, passionate husband would provide everything. All the wife had to do was cook wonderful, interesting meals, keep the house tidy and clean, and be attractive, patient, and constantly available to her husband and children. I'm trying to remember if Mom in *Father Knows Best* ever went on a trip with her girlfriends or had any challenging hobbies other than puttering around with a few flowers.

I threw myself into marriage with enthusiasm. It got me away from my father's hands and into a world I could construct for myself. I was determined not to be the cold, distant person my mother was. So I lived for my children and my husband. My time was theirs. In fifteen years, I had no life of my own. Every once in a while, I'd ask something of my husband but it got to the point where it wasn't worth it. He'd always look at me like I was being completely unreasonable, like I was asking altogether too much.

When I went into therapy he was supportive at first until I found out I had needs. Then my whole family turned against me. My husband sided with my mother, and my daughter and husband tried to talk me out of going to sessions. For the first time in my life I was getting angry and they all acted as if I was crazy.

It was hard to stay in therapy. What they did hurt a lot. For fifteen years I gave them everything in me. I gave them so much I didn't even have a self. And then when I finally started developing a me they fought me. They didn't want me to change. They wanted me to go on living just for them.

You know something? I was never revered for giving myself away. They treated me more like a brainless servant than a respected wife and mother. When I remember that it helps me keep going even though they're so against me. I'll be damned if I'll let anyone stop me now. Even if they are the people I love most in the world.

Carla's Story

Before we married, Phil couldn't get enough of me. He wanted to be with me every possible moment. He'd call me from work a couple of times a day. He'd begrudge the time I took going shopping with my girlfriends or working late to meet a deadline at my job. I felt so wanted. I didn't see a problem in it.

My dad was a drunk and my mom was a dishrag so it felt real good for someone to be so enthusiastic about me. Phil sent me flowers every week. He bought me lovely, expensive nightgowns. It turned my head.

My friends were envious. They had all been married a while and complained that even if they draped themselves nude across the TV set they couldn't get their husbands' attention, especially if a ball game was on.

Phil and I got married. Then he began criticizing my work. He said it kept me away from him. If I weren't working I could have lunch with him a couple of times a week. We could be together as soon as he got home and he'd always be able to get me when he called. (He got furious when I was away from the office with my boss and he couldn't reach me. He was jealous of my boss—this gray-haired fatherly teddy bear.)

I liked my job. I liked my boss. I liked working and having my own money, but Phil kept pressuring me so much that I finally gave in to him and quit. But then I didn't know what to do with myself, with all the time. There's only so much shopping and cooking you can do.

I made elaborate meals. Phil loved that. He'd sing my praises all night long. But even that got to be a bore. I started feeling cynical

about his enthusiasm toward me, which only made me feel like
a schmuck. Here was this man adoring me and I looked at him
sideways.

I had to do something or I'd go crazy. About that time, my priest
was talking about buying a house and fixing it up as a place for
pregnant girls to live, to give them an alternative to abortion. He
thought if we made it attractive, staffed it with good people, and
offered some kind of skills training or educational grants, the girls
could use their pregnancy as a time to get their lives together.

I loved the idea and I volunteered to work with him. When I told
Phil he was furious. I didn't get it. I reassured him that I'd be careful to work only during his working hours, that I'd be home before
he got there. But then my anger got the best of me. I told him,
"Don't worry, your gourmet meal will be on the table as usual."

He backhanded me. I couldn't believe it. I was in shock. At first
I just stared at him and then I calmly walked down the hall and
locked myself in the bathroom. He stood outside the door pleading
with me to come out. He said I was his moon and stars. He said
he'd take me out to any restaurant I wanted, it didn't matter how
expensive.

Before I would open the door, I made him promise never to hit
me again.

"I'm on my knees to you," he said. "I promise with all my
heart."

I opened the door and he was kneeling on the carpet. My heart
went out to him. No one had ever loved me so much.

So then he took me to dinner and as the waiter was clearing away
the dishes Phil took my hand. "Darling," he said. "I want you to
understand why I acted the way I did. I don't object to you working
on that project. It's a wonderful idea. But you should have talked it
over with me first. What if I'd needed your help with something?
Then you would've had to break your commitment to the priest.
From now on ask me first when you want to do something. Then
everything will be all right."

Something felt wrong with that, but it seemed like such a simple
thing. I promised I would. It wouldn't cost me anything and it was
so important to him.

For a while things were going well. Father Mike and I found a
great house and we had enough contributions to buy it. Several
families worked together to repair and paint it. Phil, of course, was

there all the time. He can do anything—wiring, plumbing, heating. I felt so proud of how willing he was to give his energies to the project. After all, this wasn't even his church originally. He converted because my church meant so much to me.

The only trouble we had was when he got home before I did. I became an expert at making it look like I'd been waiting for him to come home. Before I left in the morning I'd set the table and get dinner practically done. Sometimes I'd put it in the oven on the timer.

Many a day I'd race across town, tear into the garage, dash into the house, hide my coat in the pantry, and be tying my apron strings as he came through the front door. Then one day I discovered a curious thing. I had walked in after him, but the meat was sizzling in the oven and the house smelled delicious. I came through the door with a little bag in my hand, some horseradish I'd picked up that morning. His face had that dark look but then he saw the bag. "Oh," he said, "you had to run out for something."

I'm no fool. I said I forgot the horseradish.

He was courtly. He helped me with my coat and I went into the kitchen figuratively sweeping my hand across my brow. The next day I went to three stores and bought one thing from each place—a bag of bread crumbs, a jar of dried parsley—things I could keep in my car and take in with me if I was late again. It worked like a charm. I got the reputation with him of being a little forgetful, and he'd tell this in amusing stories to our friends, and I'd smile and think the price was worth it. I don't know why it was okay for me to be late if I forgot something and a disaster to be late if I was working at Horizon House.

A strange thing happened to me sexually. Before we were married, I was so attracted to him. Besides his dark hair and eyes, he had this passion, this enthusiasm for things. At first it was thrilling to have all that passion directed at me. When we were first married I can't even describe how it felt to see him approach me with that intense light in his eyes. I felt like the queen of the world. He's a masterful lover. It's obvious that his greatest pleasure is giving pleasure to me.

With all this, I don't understand why I began to cool. I guess it started when I quit my job. At first I felt a little removed from him. He'd caress my arm and I almost didn't feel it. I was just a little less interested in lovemaking.

When I look back it seems that it really got worse when he started telling those stories about my forgetfulness. I started faking it in bed. I had to force myself to be present.

Then another thing happened. It had to do with the mayoral election. Phil liked Ken White for mayor but I'd already decided to vote for Edgar Hambidge. So when Phil asked me about what I thought of Ken White I told him. I said I liked Edgar Hambidge. He'd done a responsible job on the school board. I said that I'd met him and felt he wasn't all wind and peanuts. His wife was a straight shooter and not one of those political wives with eyes that make you think of a dog chained to a fence. I warmed to my subject. I don't think Phil had ever asked what I thought.

I was enjoying myself so much I didn't notice what was happening to Phil's face. When his frightening glower finally registered, I changed my tune. I said, "Of course, Ken White is a very nice man."

It's odd, but I think that one sentence saved me. I couldn't tell you from what. Phil's face relaxed just a little bit and I realized I'd just made it. But from then to the election, life was a battle. Phil couldn't let a moment go by without extolling Ken White's virtues. He brought pamphlets and told stories. Believe it or not, he even took me to Ken's headquarters and introduced me to him.

At first I'd listen and say something like, "Edgar's done so-and-so." I didn't get in trouble for that, but Phil countered with 25 things Ken had done. Then three days before the election, he asked me who I was going to vote for.

I told him Edgar Hambidge and he got mad. He said, "That is so stupid. Ken White is obviously the perfect man for the job."

The next day and the day after that, he asked me again. I told the truth. Each time he got mad. By election day, he was ranting and raving and he asked me again.

I'm not proud of this, but I told him I'd decided to vote for Ken White. He was jubilant. He took me to the polls. He stopped for flowers on the way home. I never told him I'd really voted for Edgar Hambidge. And I never disagreed with him about a political candidate again, even though I continued to vote the way I wanted.

Ken White won the election. Phil told our friends that I was part of the winning team. I don't know why that got to me, but it did. I never liked people thinking I'd supported White—I think he's a crook. After that was when I really started having trouble with Phil sexually.

Father Mike asked me to help him decorate Horizon House. I love doing things like that. Father has good taste for a priest. We had the best time figuring out how to brighten up the stuff people had donated. Don't get me wrong. People were good to be so generous. But some of the stuff, let's face it, they would have had to pay to get it dragged away.

Father Mike and I decided what could be salvaged, what needed recovering, what would go where, and then we hit the stores to fill in the gaps. We picked out rugs and material for curtains and fabric for re-covering.

One day we were at Owen's department store picking out sheets. Father Mike had his arms full of bags and I was looking at him, imagining what we looked like to others. A priest in clerical collar with a young, reasonably attractive woman standing in the bedding section loading up on sheets. It struck me funny. I started laughing and so did Father Mike. For a priest, he's really fun to be with.

I got home early that day, no mad dash across town, and I was relaxed and happy as I approached the house. I walked through the door and got a fist in the head. I remember thinking as I fell that I must have surprised a burglar. So I was shocked to look up and see Phil.

"What are you doing?" I cried. "It's me!" I was thinking he thought I was a burglar.

He said, "Maybe I don't know you at all." Then he reached down, pulled me up, and struck me again. It took me several minutes to take in that he was hitting me on purpose. That he knew it was me.

Through his yelling I figured out that he'd seen us at Owen's. So I started to explain. I thought if he just knew the facts, he'd quit hitting me. Even after it dawned on me that he was jealous of Father Mike I still tried to reason with him. Then suddenly I realized that reason had nothing to do with this.

I maneuvered so that I was between him and the door and slowly backed away from him. Then I dashed out the door to my car. I had my keys in my pocket, but not my purse.

He chased me, but I got into the car and locked the door. Then he tried to close the garage door on me as I was backing out. He almost did it too. The garage door scraped the paint off the top of the car, it was that close.

At first, I just drove. I was numb. I didn't know where I was going. I was ashamed to go to Father Mike. I didn't want to tell anybody. Somehow, though—I don't know how I got there—I ended up at my best friend's house.

I was in shock, completely incapable of making a decision about what to do. It took me a couple of days to recover from the realization that my husband was beating me—that he would have shut me in a garage for having innocent fun.

My friend took care of me for a week. She hid my car in her garage and helped me find a therapist. She went with me to my first Codependents Anonymous meeting.

At one point, someone at the meeting talked about not feeling sexual toward her husband anymore. For her own protection, she had to be so guarded emotionally that she couldn't be open sexually either. I felt so relieved when she said that. That had happened to me too. It's odd but it never occurred to me to talk to my therapist about this. I'd never talked about sexual stuff with anyone. I thought there was something wrong with me that I couldn't respond to Phil when he was such an attentive lover. But now I finally understand that my body has a lot of wisdom, that it knew things were wrong in that relationship before my head did. I didn't know I should listen to my body, but now I do. It tells me I don't want to be with Phil anymore.

I've seen those movies on TV where those women stayed with their husbands for years and years, promise after broken promise, and it only got worse. I'm not going to go through all that.

Phil used both barrels to try to get me to come back—a trip to Hawaii, a new house, money for the church. He promised he would never hit me again. The women in my support group had already talked about that—the bait their husbands used to get them back— and I knew I didn't want to trade anything for my belief in myself. I saw how cowed some of those women had become, afraid of their own shadows. That's not going to happen to me.

I've lost a lot though. I think about how starry-eyed I was when I married Phil. I was so innocent. I remember being twenty and looking at women in my neighborhood in their forties and fifties. They were sort of hardened and cynical about men. They were full of warnings and I thought, you old crones, you're just that way because you don't trust anybody. I'm never going to be like that.

I'm realizing now that experience is what taught them to be that way. I look around and I don't see any woman who's forty who has the innocent enthusiasm about men she had when she was twenty. Experience has taught all of us.

You Are Me

When a couple becomes enmeshed, that is, when the individualities of each partner are sacrificed to the relationship, the individuals and the partnership suffer. Sometimes, as in Carla's case, one partner forces the other to give up separate opinions, perspectives, and preferences. Sometimes, as Donna described, a partner takes on her mate's views and ideas voluntarily.

If childhood is used for survival, then little energy is left to develop a separate sense of self. It's likely, then, that a person who had to spend childhood surviving would enter marriage as an incomplete person. She'd be vulnerable to absorbing her mate's perspectives, ideas, and attitudes and taking them as her own.

At first this might feel good to both partners. She'd feel stronger now that she had some ideas she hadn't had before. He'd feel very important that he could give her these things and that she liked them enough to take them on—very flattering. What would happen later, though, when she disagreed with him? It would upset the balance of the marriage. She'd be changing a pattern that had been established. He might feel she was attacking his way of thinking.

Who's Really Running Things

Another subtle shift happens when one person in the relationship sees himself as setting the limits and doing the thinking. He begins to see himself as more powerful and valuable. Anyone who's worked in supportive services has experienced this.

When I worked in a hospital I was very aware of who really ran the place—the nurses. They kept track of continuity, they knew what was really going on, they were tuned in to the patients, they kept the operation functioning. Who got the pay and the esteem? The doctors. They'd run in, see four patients in an hour, scribble some things on the chart, and leave. They had the power to make decisions, the ultimate liability (and high insurance fees), and got the glory and the money.

Who runs the office?—the secretaries. I haven't talked to my insurance agent for two years. His secretary is the one who updates the policies, issues new ones, figures out my rates. Who gets the money? The insurance agent. Who thinks he's most important? The insurance agent. He hired the secretary. He issues her orders as he dashes out to lunch.

The same phenomenon happens in marriages. If one partner is set up to do the thinking and make the decisions, that partner (let's say the husband) will see himself as more powerful and important, even if his wife is the one who keeps the show going. This imbalance can cause the supportive partner to feel less and less important, less sure of her value and the worth of her ideas, more dependent on her husband, and more enmeshed.

In many marriages, the man is perceived as the head of the household and the woman as the partner who submits. I thought this died out some time ago, but I was wrong. Many women still enter into marriages in which both husband and wife believe the man does the thinking and the woman follows along. Some use the Bible to back this up.

The Bible says the man is the *spiritual* head of the household and it delineates clearly the man's responsibilities to his wife (Ephesians 5:25–33), not just hers to him. I've noticed that when men thump their Bibles over this matter, they seem to forget that their own job description is contained there. The Bible does not say that women are supposed to stop thinking. In fact, all the memorable women in the Bible were thinkers, opinionated, sometimes argumentative, often unafraid to challenge even God.

An Enmeshed Person Is Not Known

Obviously, too much distance in a relationship leads to a cooling of romantic interest. Surprisingly, enmeshment can do the same. Here's why. Enmeshment, remember, may feel close, but it isn't. Enmeshment means someone's individuality is being squashed. An enmeshed person is not known.

Phil seemed intensely involved with Carla. The truth is, however, he did not know her. He did not want her thoughts to be on anything but him. He wanted her opinions to echo his. He wanted to control her decisions and strove actively to separate her from people, work, and ideas that might take her attention from him. This kind of compulsive focus on a person is misleading. At first Carla felt she was the center of Phil's world. The truth that emerged, however, is that Phil's *image* of Carla was the center of his world and whenever the real person deviated from that image she was rejected. No wonder she lost the ability to feel his touch. He wasn't touching Carla. He was touching his image of Carla.

True intimacy, in which each person is well known, leads to emotional closeness and easily into physical closeness.

Phil's Story

When I married Carla, I thought I'd captured the sweetest flower on the face of the earth. She was so fresh and pink and shy. Nothing like my mother, who could stop a Sherman tank if she'd a mind to.

She loved to hear me talk. I admit it, I liked it. When had my parents ever listened to me?

I worshipped her. She was like a queen to me—the utmost in feminine grace. I wanted to buy her everything. I wanted to give her fancy clothes, the best house, anything she wanted.

She didn't need to work. Why should she use herself up in a job that didn't matter? I make three times what she can make. She can stay home and I'll take care of her. I don't need much. A hot meal when I get home. To walk through the door and see her lovely face. I wait all day for that. Is it so much to ask?

Really, that's all I wanted from her. To be home when I got there. To have dinner ready. To let me make love to her. Someone please explain to me what is wrong with this.

Don't you understand how much I love her? I love her more than life itself. I would gladly give my life for her.

I never meant to hit her. I wanted to cut off my hand after I did it. It horrified me. I'm not one of those men who thinks his wife deserves a beating.

I would like you to understand my side though. I had dropped into Owen's to pick up a present for her. My every thought is on her. I'm absolutely faithful to her. I wouldn't even look at another woman.

Anyway, I was headed to the lingerie section—that's on the other side of linens and bedding. I glanced over there and saw this beautiful woman laughing. She was so merry and I thought how lucky the man with her was, to bring such joy to his woman. When I saw it was Carla, I went crazy. Doesn't anyone understand that? I would buy Kentucky if I could put such a look on Carla's face. Another man, even a priest, giving that to her? No. I couldn't bear it. She's mine and mine only.

I don't understand the problem over the election. I was just trying to prevent Carla from making a mistake. She doesn't know these guys like I do. Ken White's a member of my club. He's a great guy. It's good for us to know people in office.

I don't believe she's lost interest in lovemaking. When we married, she was incredible—fresh, innocent, and passionate too. I have to express my love for her in every way, physically as well as through words and actions.

The therapist asked me if I knew how Carla thought, if I knew what her interests were. I can answer that. She likes a clean house. She likes to cook. She likes to be attractive for me. She's a real lady, in the good old-fashioned sense. She likes to be active.

She's a wonderful hostess. Anyone could tell you what fun they had when they came to our house for dinner. She knows how to put people at ease, makes them feel welcome. I was always very proud to be with her. We had lots of wonderful evenings, just the two of us. I'd read or talk, she'd do needlework and listen. What was it you asked? About her interests. Right. She likes to entertain and to do handwork.

You want me to tell you more about her? What does it matter? What matters is that I love her. I'd do anything for her. That's the most important thing in the world. Nothing else counts.

Can This Marriage Be Saved?

Maybe. It's always a problem in a relationship if a person holds one strict view and can't take in an alternative perspective. It's comfortable to believe there's only one way to look at things and that nothing beyond that view exists. If Phil doesn't know about it, it doesn't exist. Period. He may truly love Carla enough to break his tightly held pattern, or he may find another woman to worship and continue through life in the dark about himself.

Their relationship illustrates well the difference between enmeshed involvement and true intimacy.

So the closeness desired in a committed relationship includes physical and emotional intimacy, knowing each other very well, understanding the other's thought processes, and an awareness of differences and similarities in perspective, opinion, attitude, preference, ideals, values, and goals. This intimacy includes the freedom to disagree, to want something different, and to have different needs.

What about too much difference? What is too much distance in a committed relationship?

Lack of Intimacy Means I Am Not Known

One cause of too much distance comes from not talking about important matters. If intimacy means being known by the other, lack of intimacy comes about from not being known. If partners aren't talking about problems, feelings, needs, and wants, they'll feel less known, and distance will grow between them.

Distance also results when a partner is cold or emotionally withdrawn, when he makes himself unavailable to his partner, when he's focused primarily on work or alcohol or chemicals or acquiring things or getting ahead, or when he lets stress mount so high that he can't come out of himself to see the other.

Why would a husband be cold to his wife? If, as a boy, he was taught to disregard feelings, then he was taught to be out of touch with himself. Remember, emotional boundaries develop as we know ourselves and our feelings. If a child is taught to ignore his inner self, his inner self won't develop.

How can a man come home from the office and pour out his anxieties if he's not been taught to be in touch with them? That part of himself was walled off long ago. He may not even know it exists.

To Feel or Not to Feel

Women often do handstands trying to get men to talk about their feelings. But they might as well be speaking Swahili for all the good it does. They may get very emotional and thus remind the men exactly why they swore off feelings in the first place—they're messy; they make you lose control. To feel or not to feel becomes an enormous power struggle, a struggle that polarizes many a man and woman.

Boy children are often taught their worth resides in what they can do, not who they are. Their focus is doing, not being, and they grow up taking refuge in doing.

When a person neither knows his feelings nor has healthy ways to handle them, he is vulnerable to whatever will keep his feelings contained—alcohol, drugs, food, excessive work, stress, compulsive acquiring, compulsive hobbying.

What's the solution? Getting expert help to learn the skills not learned as children. Therapists, classes, and anonymous programs all offer ways to discover one's hidden self, constructive ways to get back in contact with feelings. With support, you can safely feel hard things—without crashing or hurting someone else—until you're ready to solo.

A wife is not the best person to teach her husband how to feel. The other issues in the marriage will sabotage the process and neither one will emerge enlightened.

Your Rooms and Mine

Distance in a relationship can also result if the partners are very different from one another. It takes excellent communication and very clear boundaries to have intimacy when many differences exist.

(Although, if you're scared of intimacy, pick someone very different from you. Distance will be built in and the ensuing struggles will keep you both very busy. You'll be so involved you won't know you don't have intimacy.)

If your guiding light in life is to gather as many possessions as possible and mine is to live simply without dependence on things, we would have to have very intact boundaries to keep this difference from causing trouble in the relationship. Your things could threaten the space I need to feel comfortable.

We might need to divide the house between your rooms and mine, so that we could each be free to arrange our visual and physical space to suit our needs. We would each have to work at accepting that your values are perfectly okay and have nothing to do with mine, and that mine are fine and say nothing about you.

Intimacy Takes a Lot of Work

Marriage or a committed partnership permits the greatest physical and emotional intimacy. This intimacy comes about as partners grow in their knowledge and acceptance of each other. The balance between appropriate closeness and distance is difficult to find.

With too much distance, the couple begins to lead separate lives in separate worlds. They develop separate languages and constituents. Sexual fulfillment decreases.

With enmeshment, at least one person's separateness is lost. The other person may lose respect. Both may lose track of the other's uniqueness. Sexual fulfillment decreases.

Thus marriage is a process that challenges two people to develop their individuality in the context of intimacy. This process is delicate, difficult, and deliberate. The myth is that when the vows are spoken, intimacy automatically locks in place and leads you forward, like those automated trams at airports. The truth is that intimacy takes a lot of work and must be deliberately undertaken. I'll have more about intimacy in Chapter Eight.

Friendships

What is the appropriate range of closeness between friends? In one sense, the sky's the limit. A friendship may be based on going to the movies together once a month or sharing the darkest secrets a couple of times a day.

Great emotional closeness is possible between friends. As in marriage, the keys to closeness are communication and being known. Sometimes physical closeness becomes a part of the friendship. Friends may hug and hold each other in a nonsexual way that gives warmth and comfort.

Sexual intimacy (not just sexual actions but speaking of one's sexual attraction to the other) generally changes the boundaries of the relationship. Sex that is not prepared for with emotional intimacy leaves a gap. Unless the gap is filled with increasing emotional closeness, the relationship and possibly the participants will suffer.

The sexual revolution, a reaction to America's abiding Victorianism, extended sexual contact into casual acquaintance. Strictures against sexuality were once so encompassing that women weren't supposed to enjoy sex even after marriage. They certainly weren't supposed to talk about it.

The pendulum has swung so far in the opposite direction that high school children are being sexual with partners they barely know.

One consequence of AIDS is that we've had to learn about sexual responsibility the hard way. We now see that sexual experience brings about bonding, and hurt comes from bonding with people who will continue to be casual about us.

So friendship offers a tremendous range of acceptable closeness and distance. A relationship will move in the direction of increased closeness if the participants make themselves known and make themselves open to knowing the other.

Physical intimacy can be sexual and nonsexual. Nonsexual physical intimacy can be nurturing and comforting. Sexual intimacy changes the dynamic of the relationship. If emotional intimacy and the ability to communicate clearly about hard things has preceded it, it can enhance the relationship. If sexual intimacy is not grounded in emotional closeness and effective communication, it can lead to problems in the relationship.

Parents and Children

Children need a lot from their parents beyond food, clothing, shelter, safety, and security. They need parental interest, guidance, affection, concern, and safe physical contact.

Parental attention develops boundaries. Interest in a child's activities helps the child value what she can do. Interest in a child's thoughts helps the child expand his sense of his own mental processes. Guidance helps the child realize that certain choices are superior to others—an essential aspect of boundary development. Concern communicates a boundary—that the child is nearing a limit. Physical affection communicates that the child belongs, that he or she is part of a unit. It helps the child develop the boundary of us and not-us.

Both too much distance and too much closeness between parents and children lead to problems. To a child, too much distance means abandonment and emotional neglect. Too much closeness—enmeshment—prevents the child from developing his own individuality and can foster in him a feeling of being responsible for the well-being of his parents.

Distance Makes the Heart Grow Colder

Why are some people emotionally distant? Why would parents, especially, be distant from their children? Why would a father look to his daughter to meet his needs? Isn't it clear that she needs him?

People can require great emotional distance or enmeshment for a number of reasons—parental influence, chemical dependence, high stress, unmet needs, or inability to protect oneself.

We Raise Children the Way We Were Raised

Parents are likely to parent as they were parented unless they've learned a different way and had their own needs met. How can a parent create intimacy if he's only known distance? How can she set limits if she's only known enmeshment?

Intimacy requires that we know our feelings and needs, that we communicate them, and that we understand how to get our needs met. We must know how to work out disagreements, how to handle anger, how to have balance, and be able to respect the different needs, feelings, thoughts, and reactions of another. With either distant or enmeshing parents, our experience is limited when it comes to learning these skills.

Distant parents provide too little emotional contact. Children receive insufficient mirroring, guidance, closeness, or feedback to develop a sense of their emotional selves. A child of enmeshed parents, on the other hand, gets filled, not with her own feelings, thoughts, and values, but with theirs.

When such children become parents themselves, they tend to parent either in a similar fashion or reactively. For example, a daughter of withdrawn parents might become a distant mother or she might get overinvolved in her children's lives. She might want so much to protect them from the coldness she felt growing up that she unwittingly gets enmeshed with them, therefore depriving them of their separateness.

When we become parents we are vulnerable to being copies of our parents, the opposite of them, or some complicated combination of the two.

Laura's Story

From the time I was a small girl, I was trained to meet the needs of others. My grandmother spent huge amounts of time doing volunteer work for worthwhile charities. In fact, she was gone a lot as I was growing up.

From watching her and because I was so alone I learned early that I existed to serve others. My job in particular was to meet my mother's needs. I was to protect her and keep her secrets from my grandparents.

When I got pregnant, I could think only of what the baby would give me. I thought of her as being something for me, someone who would be mine, who would provide me with a family. It was a lot to expect of someone who weighed less than a bag of apples.

She died at birth, but I can see now what kind of parent I would have become. I would have expected her to meet my needs. At that time in my life I'd been exposed to no information about effective parenting, even though I had a good education and did well in school.

I can see that I'd have said things like, "Not now, later." "Don't bother me, can't you see I'm busy?" "Get me my cigarettes." I can see I'd have felt pressured by her needs. I couldn't get mine met. How the hell could I have met hers?

It's Not the Child's Job

How can parents meet the emotional needs of their children if their own go unmet? Some parents do a remarkable job despite this, but it's like pushing a boulder uphill. Many of these parents sacrifice themselves for their children. Others sacrifice their children for themselves. Children of a constantly sacrificing parent may repeat that same role when they become parents, passing on the sacrificial model and the resentment that invariably accompanies it.

Parents may use their children to get their own needs met. Here are some of the ways parents use their children.

1. Expecting the child to take care of the parent.

    Parents may expect a child to take care of them emotionally, to listen to adult problems, or to give them encouragement or comfort.

    It's lovely if a child has the natural capacity to occasionally offer comfort, but it is not the child's full-time job.

2. Asking the child to make adult decisions.

    Children are sometimes presented with choices that are an adult's to make. A child made to feel responsible for the well-being of her parents is forced into a role she is ill-equipped to handle. She knows this and can grow up feeling too responsible for everything and inadequate to handle so much.

3. Enmeshing with the child—either living life vicariously by becoming too involved with the child's thoughts, interests, and activities or making the child into a clone of the parent.

    Enmeshment, then, can arise from a parent's desperate feeling of emptiness. Mom wants to be filled and she fills herself with the child's life.

    Enmeshment can also be a way to feel validated. The child is made into a photocopy of the parent's interests and values, so that the parent's choices are reinforced. Dad is a lion tamer so his son must be a lion tamer. The family has always eaten peanuts so the daughter has to eat peanuts.

4. Misusing the child in order to feel powerful or to express anger.

    Incest can result when a parent needs to feel powerful. It can be a way of expressing anger at one's spouse or at all people of that gender. Physically abusing a child is another way to handle anger or frustration or feelings of being trapped and overwhelmed. The parent beats the child to relieve his or her emotional needs.

Children Are Supposed to Have Needs

Children need a lot. They come into the world with a set of demands. If a parent is already overwhelmed with his own unmet needs, the child's needs are just too much. Parents can handle this onslaught of demands by squashing them—verbally or physically abusing the child to get him to stop demanding—or by being very distant, becoming so cold and withdrawn that the child's demands go unheard. Then the child suffers neglect and abandonment; she may grow up denying her own needs and later insist that her children meet them.

It's an intricate, entangled cycle. The harm can be stopped, however, if parents enter into therapy or some form of treatment or recovery that will teach them healthy ways to handle their feelings and get their needs met.

I was very sad in a recent session with parents. The father was using his son in a power struggle with his wife. The father decided he wasn't willing to stay in therapy to learn to be a different parent. Not only is he likely to lose his wife and family, he is also passing on to his son a legacy that will affect not only his entire life but the lives of his son's children. Two or more generations affected because a father is afraid to feel.

Our Drug of Choice Comes First

Dependence on a chemical or compulsion can be another cause of too much distance in a relationship. If we are addicted to a substance or dependent on a compulsion, we need very wide boundaries. We can't let anyone near who might interfere with our use or take our supply.

If I need to work compulsively and you demand time from me, time I want to use working, I'll have to keep you at a distance. Otherwise, you'll take my supply of time and energy needed for working. If I need to eat sugar and you call as I'm on my way to the kitchen, I'll have to get rid of you so I can get my fix.

ı put people at a distance by being cold and unresponsive, by giving sharp, short answers, by discounting them and their needs. We can refuse to talk about our feelings, refuse to talk about important issues, or refuse to listen to them.

When a person needs a chemical or an activity, he must keep away people who would interfere with his use. He must protect his supply, protect his intake, protect the secrecy around his need to use.

A child becomes very peripheral to the need for the drug. A child becomes something to get out of the way.

A Child Keeps On Needing No Matter What You're Going Through

Stress can cause people to need greater distance from others. If we are very burdened by work, fear, bills, illness, or unmet needs, we may be less available to listen and give. Unfortunately, a child keeps right on needing no matter what you're going through. You need to find a way to pay the bills, he needs to tell you about his game.

Sometimes we experience more stress than the situation requires. Generally, stress means we aren't getting enough help. It can be heightened by self-made rules about doing things perfectly and not making any mistakes, by black and white thinking, not accepting help, not getting advice, not trusting, thinking we have to do everything ourselves, and other rules we may have made to survive childhood.

Sometimes we get hooked on stress. Perhaps it's the intensity. Perhaps the rush makes us high. We have the sharpness of the hunter and the hunted.

Meanwhile, a child may be standing within range, needing, but invisible to us. Get out of the way, child, I must focus on this, not you. This involves money. It's the most important thing in the world. I'll get to you when I'm done here.

But if we're addicted to stress, or dependent on the rules that keep our lives stressful, we may never get around to the child. We look up and the child is on drugs or beating a sister or grown up with no reason to bring the grandchildren to visit.

Certain Lines Should Not Be Crossed

Context defines the range of closeness and distance appropriate within a relationship. Behavior that is completely acceptable in one context can be unhealthy and even harmful in a different type of relationship.

We don't have a scale that measures degrees of intimacy so ranges cannot be precisely defined. Certain lines, however, should not be crossed. Children should not be used to meet the sexual or power needs of parents. Children shouldn't have to solve adult problems. Too much distance can kill a marriage. And every one of us has a choice about how much of ourselves we will reveal to people we don't know well.

If you get confused sometimes about what is appropriate with another person, think about the type of relationship it is. Consider if the behavior is within the bounds of the relationship. Chapter Four will help you strengthen your emotional boundaries. As you develop a clearer sense of self, your instincts will help you know what feels right and what feels wrong in a relationship.

Your Parents' Boundaries

Exercise 3.1

Whatever mishmash of boundaries your parents had profoundly influenced your development. The purpose of this exercise is to identify these influences.

Part I.   Pick a parent, your mother or father or other adult, and answer the following questions.
1. In what ways was your parent distant or withdrawn from you? Include
   a. Incidents in which you ran to your parent with enthusiasm and he or she turned you away without following up on your excitement
   b. Events missed, such as no one there when you were the lion in the school play
   c. Broken promises
   d. Evidence that your preferences were unknown
   e. Evidence that your thought processes were not understood
   f. Evidence that your interests were missed
   g. Being passed over when something concerned the whole family

2. In what ways was your parent enmeshed with you? Include
   a. Ideas held by the parent that were forced on you
   b. Preferences that a parent expected you to share
   c. Evidence that your parent assumed you felt the way he or she did
   d. Parental ways which you were expected to adopt
3. In what ways did your parent use you to meet his or her needs? Include needs for
   a. Power
   b. Comfort
   c. Sex
   d. Stress relief
   e. Solution of adult problems
   f. Other

Part II. Repeat this exercise with any other person who assumed a parental role towards you.

Part III. From what you know of your grandparents on both sides, what's your best guess about their boundaries? Write about each grandparent. Identify suspected patterns of enmeshment, withdrawal, coldness, intrusion, and the expectation that children existed to meet their needs.

CHAPTER FOUR

YOUR PHYSICAL BOUNDARIES

You Have Absolute Say Over Who Touches You

Absolute! You are the guardian of your own body. You are the one who monitors how close each person can get. You determine how you are touched.

Your life is yours. You are the one accountable for your choices. You bear the consequences of your decisions and your body bears the consequences of your decisions about it. You choose what to eat, how much to exercise, how completely to rest. The care of your body is in your hands and you are the one who lives with the results. If you decide to floss your teeth, you get to enjoy healthy gums. If you decide to live in a way that keeps you driven and tense, you are the one who lives with high blood pressure, greater susceptibility to illness, and strained relationships.

Where are your boundaries? Where do others stop and you begin? Your skin is your physical boundary. You also monitor the personal space that you keep between you and others.

You need not suffer the lack of awareness of a stranger who comes too close. But you are in charge of seeing that people stay at a comfortable distance. You can back up, or stand so that something is between you and the other person. Or you can stick out your arm and say "No closer, please," or "You may want to back up. If I breathe on you, you'll be sick for a month."

The only exception is if you are incapacitated and must receive medical attention. Beyond this, you have the right to say who touches you and how.

Why am I belaboring this? Why am I as impassioned as a mother writing to her daughter at college? Because I continue to see evidence that even women believe a woman's body is not her own.

Bodies for Sale

On a recent trip to Florida, I was astounded at the bikinis I saw. In the Northwest, where I live, it's so cold and rainy that bikini wearing would threaten the species. I hadn't realized a fabric shortage was hitting the rest of the country and that swim suits were being sacrificed to make up for it. But then having personal boundaries means that within the law a person can wear as little as he or she wants.

I was saddened, though, that women of all ages felt they had to suffer such a garment, because the obvious purpose of such a suit is to sell one's body to another. It couldn't be comfortable to lie on the sand with no more protection than a cocktail napkin.

Many ads for cosmetics, perfume, clothing, and hygiene items convey that a woman's job is to be pleasing to others. The fortunes we spend on these products demonstrate that at least in part women swallow this message. One's natural body is not good enough; we need cloth and potions to remedy what we're taught to perceive as defects.

A Rude Comment Says Nothing About Us

When a person with extra weight decides not to do something from fear of ridicule, he's living the idea that he can't enjoy himself if others don't find his body attractive. I'm angered at the agonies my clients suffer because extra weight exposes them to rude comments. They believe they are inferior because of some pounds on their bodies. They don't go swimming. They deprive themselves of rafting trips because they're scared to go up to a counter and not find a wet suit in their size. They consider missing a reunion because people will see them in a larger size than they wore at the last one. They hesitate to go to a dance or a wedding because compared to magazine models they see themselves as inferior.

Every one of my clients is beautiful. Every one of them is extremely valuable to this earth, with wonderful qualities, rich awarenesses, unique gifts. It infuriates me that worship of appearance in this country has reached so extreme a degree that these women deprive themselves of a full life because of the ignorance of others.

A rude comment from a stranger says nothing about us. It says a lot about the stranger. If cousin Mildred makes her usual snide remark at a family picnic ("She shouldn't really wear shorts"), I don't have to put up with it. I can set her straight and walk away with my head held high. To paraphrase Goethe, "Cousin Mildred, when ideas fail, words come in very handy."

Your Body Is Yours

So I am impassioned. I want you to enjoy your life. I want you to go where you want and do the things you want to do. Use your money to expand your life and your health rather than on the pursuit of appearance.

I want you to enjoy the safety of knowing that your skin, your body, is yours and no one else's and that you determine how it is to be treated. You live with your body. You die with your body. It takes you where you want to go and is the vehicle within which you travel the world. You have absolute ownership of your body.

If you don't want someone to touch you, if you don't want to be hugged, you get to say so. If someone you don't like puts an arm around your shoulders, you get to move away. You do not have to endure any kind of contact you don't want.

The law backs this up. In this country it's a felony for someone to harm your body. If someone injures you, takes your life, or is sexual against your will, it is a crime.

What about extreme cases? What if we're forced to endure someone's touch? Obviously we are not at fault for this. When threatened with harm or injury, we may have to submit to unwanted contact.

Most of the time, however, we can enforce our right to determine who touches us. Anytime we let someone touch us when we don't want to be touched, unless we are overpowered, we let that person commit a crime against us. It's harmful for us. It's harmful for the other guy.

When a boss comes too close, for example, we may feel we have little choice but to endure it. Look at the consequences, though, of putting up with it. An unwanted hand is on my body. My natural response is to move away, remove his hand, and spit in his face. Instead I smile sweetly and pretend I don't notice what he's doing. I give my body the message that its natural instincts don't count and tell my feelings, pipe down, my need for money is greater than my need for self-protection. I'm teaching myself that my body is a tool that others get to use regardless of what I want, that others are allowed access to it even if I don't want them to have it. I am diminished. My acquiescence steals some iron from my soul and makes me weaker.

What happens to my boss? He learns what he already knew, that women are for him to enjoy and that power allows one to use others. Like Andrew Young says, "Nothing is illegal if a hundred businessmen decide to do it." He is enabled in pleasing himself at the expense of someone else, but he too is diminished.

Donna's Story

The longer I've been in therapy, the madder my husband's gotten. But he doesn't express his anger directly. Instead he withholds what I need from him, he withdraws, and he complains about me to my mother.

I wish he'd just stomp into the house, yell about his anger and fear and get it out in the open.

Because of what my father did, sex is very hard for me. I need to go real slow. I need a lot of touching and holding first.

I was so lonely when I was a kid. My mom cold and focused only on work, my dad using my body but never there for my inner self. I wonder if you could begin to imagine how alone I felt. I got involved with boys young. I just wanted someone to hold me. I was desperate for affection.

I still am. Even now, I really just have sex so I can get held for a while.

In the evenings, I'll sit down by my husband and he'll move away. He's always done this, even before he got so mad at me. In all the years we've been married I must have told him at least 200 times how much I want to be held. I ask him to put his arm around me. I ask him to hug me.

But whenever he holds me, it isn't a minute before his hands are roving and he's starting sex. No matter how much I explain that sometimes I need holding without sex, he doesn't get it.

I came back from therapy the other night and my face was red and swollen. It was obvious I'd been crying. I came in and he said, "Come here, Baby."

For one ecstatic minute I thought he was going to comfort me. But no sooner am I sitting down than he's pawing me. He's rubbing his hands over my body like I'm not inside it. I was so vulnerable from my session and so stunned by what he was doing that I couldn't do anything. I can't seem to stop someone from using me.

I looked in his face and I didn't see love. He was angry. He was angry and he was using sex to handle his anger at me.

I couldn't stop him. I felt guilty for having so many problems. I felt responsible because he doesn't get all the sex he wants. So I let him use my body to vent his anger.

Later I felt terrible. I felt like a piece of meat. How can a man invade a woman and not give a shit for what it does to her?

Using Hurts the User Too

Anyone who has been through this knows how degrading it is to be used as an object or tool. But it hurts the user. It gives him permission to abuse another human being. In the end, both lose pieces of themselves.

Not for a second do I think Donna is totally responsible for this. Her husband has responsibility as the sexualizer, the depersonalizer, the abuser. But since it is her body, it's up to her to protect herself from physical, sexual, and emotional harm if someone else abdicates responsibility for behaving decently.

Sometimes it isn't possible. Sometimes our childhood sets us up to be defenseless.

Essie's Story

All the years I was married I felt like I was climbing a mountain with sides that slipped every step I took. I can't remember when I didn't feel overwhelmed or bewildered. I've always been a person who tries real hard so I'm surprised when I try so hard that nothing's left inside me and everything's just the same as it was before I started.

Now I can't even remember why I married Hal. I was young and I wanted to get away from home. I wanted something of my own. I wanted to belong to someone.

So I let him carry me off. What did I know about him? He wanted me, and that was enough for me. It felt very good to be wanted.

I rolled up my sleeves. My only concern was to please him. I shopped at St. Vincent's and turned bright cloth into cheery curtains. I scrubbed down his apartment, which was filthy when I moved in. I did the recipe routine.

He lived as he pleased, and I learned not to question him. Whenever I wanted something from him or asked him anything, he'd always turn it around so that it'd be me wanting too much or me being stupid. It was very subtle.

I remember the first year we were married, after we moved into our first house. I invited my family over for a barbecue on Mother's Day. Hal went camping the day before and said he'd be back. My family kept arriving and they'd ask, "Where's Hal?"

"I don't know," I answered again and again. "He went camping at Fall Creek. He's supposed to be back."

I had prepared everything, wanting it all to be perfect. I had a home finally. I was an adult, married, with a home. I was a hostess. The barbecue was an important symbol for me and one I wanted to show my family.

We waited. And waited. Finally we went ahead with the barbecue, me making apologies. "I don't know why he isn't here. I'm sorry he isn't here." He never did show up. My family left. Then he came home.

"I drove by a couple times. I didn't want to face your family so I played basketball down the street."

I just shut my mouth, cleaned up, and felt bad. I thought he might notice I was unhappy and say he was sorry, but he never did. I waited lots of times for him to notice me.

He smoked a lot. In winter, he'd fill the house with smoke. I'd get sick from it. If I opened a window, he'd ridicule me. "What's the matter with you. It's all in your mind. It's not even smoky in here. Damn it, Essie, shut that window! You make such a big deal out of a little thing."

He was gone a lot. I never knew where he was. He never took me anywhere. I'd stay home and wait for him.

He might come back home after a couple of hours or be gone till the middle of the night. Mostly he was gone. I got real careful about how I talked to him. I'd approach what I needed to know on tiptoe. "Hal, I'm just planning supper and I need to know how much to make. Did you want supper tonight?"

"Just don't make it then."

I'd fix something, thinking that's what a wife is supposed to do. He wouldn't come home. I'd wait, keep it warm, try to keep it good. He'd shuffle in late at night.

"Dinner is wrecked," I'd say.

"What's your problem? I work hard. I can go out if I want to." He'd sit down to eat and complain because it was tough or dried up.

I never understood why he wouldn't come home. He never said why. I just thought I must not be very pleasant to be with.

He used drugs a lot. I didn't know much about drugs. We never had any money.

He went from job to job. "They" were always the reason he had to leave one job and look for another. He made up stories about why things didn't work. In the end, he lost his jobs because he was always late and always arranging for a fix instead of working. He'd get another job and then wouldn't get up in the morning. I'd try to get him up.

"Don't worry so much. I'll take care of it. Just leave me alone. If you think you can do any better, do it yourself. I'm trying and you're making me lose my confidence."

We had to move out of the house because we couldn't keep up the rent. My father let us use an apartment in a building he owned. I started working two jobs to hold things together.

Every twinge of discontent I saw in him, I tried to fix. I tried to create a nice home so that he would love me.

He came home one night and there wasn't any food because we didn't have any money. He had just gotten out of a treatment center and we were poor and trying to get back on our feet. I was tired all the time from working so hard and trying to keep up with what he wanted. He turned over the refrigerator, trashed the apartment, and put his hand through a mirror.

I got up and cleaned it all up. The next day he said he didn't remember any of it. "Why do you make up these things, Essie? The place looks just like it always does."

"That's because I cleaned it up after you trashed the place."

No comment and out the door he'd go. If I complained, he'd leave.

On our anniversary, I made dinner. The candle melted all the way down to the plate. Of course, he didn't show up.

When I had a glimmer he didn't love me, I tried harder. I thought if I tried hard enough I could make a marriage. He just needed lots of love. If I loved him enough and gave him enough of what he wanted, he'd love me.

There was one crisis after another, but he could always give a reason for it. I knew when to stop talking so he wouldn't hit me.

No matter what he did, I could always see the needy little boy inside him. He needed drugs to make up for me not filling him up.

I was so compliant. I kept trying to do what he wanted. He didn't start hitting me till the end when I got angry.

One day after Mara died, I was standing beneath him and he spit on me. I was so angry, I picked up a shovel and threw it toward him. I wasn't really trying to hit him. I just wanted to show him how angry I was. Then I got the animals in the car and started to drive away. He threw a boulder through the window. He didn't care that he could have seriously injured me or the animals.

We'd have these big violent scenes and then afterwards a calm where he was apologetic and tearful. I would see this starved little boy who didn't mean to do these awful things. He'd plead, "I care about you. I'll try harder." He'd do enough to get me to stay.

I took out a loan for treatment after he attempted suicide. During treatment he would open up and show me his inner thoughts and feelings. I responded so fully to him when he did that. The day he came out of treatment, he was secretive again and concealed what he was doing. When I questioned him, he said, "Don't you trust me?"

He was in treatment four times. In between, he'd come home really late and sleep in a tent in the backyard. He said I wrecked aftercare for him because I didn't trust him. He'd walk in with his eyes red and I'd think maybe I am crazy. Maybe I'm so afraid he's using I'm creating this in my mind.

He came home from aftercare group one day and said he never did love me but he married me because I was going to college and he knew he could always count on me to take care of him. He said I'd enabled him so much it was my fault that he'd drugged.

The worst time of all was when Mara was born. I woke and my water had broken. Hal said, "No, it can't be now. I'm sick. I can't do this."

I felt utterly helpless. "It can't be now? It is now. Do you think I can hold the baby inside until you're ready? I have to go to the hospital." It was eight in the morning.

We got in the car. He said, "I've got to make a stop."

He went a ways north of the city. The hospital was downtown. He went to the house of someone he knew. At the door he said, "My wife is in labor. I need $50 to make a deposit so she can get in the hospital."

He brought the man to the car. It was like a weird scene out of a movie. Here's the wife. See she's pregnant. The wife smiled. See, I'm pregnant. I was willing to play along, do anything so he'd take me to the hospital.

The man gave him $50. He drove back toward the city and then past the turn to the hospital and kept going south. "Hal, take me to the hospital."

"I've got to see someone."

I was so frightened and so helpless. I felt desperate to get to the hospital. I felt desperate to get some care, to be with people who would help me.

He drove to a dealer's house. The dealer got in the car. He drove to a fast food place and waited behind it. We were waiting for two Mexican guys to show up. I was so scared. When you're in pain, a minute is a really long time. Plus, I didn't know how long this was going to go on.

The guys finally came. Hal got out of the car with the dealer, stood with the guys, and then went into the restroom. When he came back, his eyes were half shut. I didn't know if he could even drive like that. I was afraid he would drift off and not know what he was doing.

Then he had to take the dealer back to his house. It was after noon before we finally got to the hospital. I had called the hospital before we left the apartment. What took so long, they wondered. They were expecting me long before we got there.

I was told to walk around until my body was at the point I should go into the labor room. Hal was upset that he couldn't smoke. As we were walking, Hal kept going into the bathroom to smoke or dope. He needed a fix every two hours. I stood in the hall hoping no one would come by. I was still covering for him, hiding this from my dad and family. He was stealing the knobs off the bathrooms. Planning to sell it for dope later, I guess. I was so ashamed. I didn't want anyone to know it was like this.

I was in labor 36 hours. He kept coming in to get my checkbook so he could buy more dope. He couldn't stand to be with me in the labor room. I was so alone. He wasn't with me. As my family arrived, they'd ask, "Where's Hal?"

I'd cover for him. I didn't want to say he's out getting more dope.

When Mara was transferred to the children's hospital, he wasn't there. I had an infection and had to stay in the central hospital and my baby was miles away in another hospital.

While I was in there, he totaled my car, hocked the TV, and got money from everybody. The people at my work, janitors, maids, people who work hard and don't make much, took up a collection for me. $1000. A lot of money for them to give and I needed it desperately. I hid it, but he found it and spent it.

When I visited her, I had to go by wheelchair. Hal couldn't figure out renting or borrowing a wheelchair, so he stole one from the hospital.

She died and I wanted time alone with her before the funeral. I was at home, ready to go, and Hal had disappeared again with my car. I needed to get to the funeral home. Finally I called his dad and asked him to come for me. Later, Hal walked into the home with a cigarette. I despised him then. How disrespectful he was to our daughter.

I never felt the same about him again. It was the first time I absolutely could not take care of him, that I needed him to pull himself together and he couldn't do it.

After seven years of this, I had finally had it. I began sneaking things out of the house. When he caught on, he smashed my wood carvings and my trophies that I won when I was a kid and traded my jewelry-making and leather-working tools for dope.

I came home one day and all my furniture was gone. Everything I owned. My wedding ring and a gold piece my grandmother had given me, gone.

Every time I stood up for myself he hurt me.

It's hard for me to talk about what I went through because someone always says, "Why did you put up with this? Why didn't you walk out on him?"

Then I feel ashamed that I stayed with him so long and kept trying so hard. I couldn't defend myself against him and I still have a hard time defending myself against comments like that. I always feel I should have done better.

No matter what a person does to me, I have the hardest time believing the person is bad or mean. I always can think of reasons for what the person does.

He can't help it. He doesn't mean to be thoughtless. He just gets so caught up in what he's doing, he doesn't realize the effect it has on me.

It took hearing my therapist say a thousand times, "Driving all over the city for four hours when you're in pain and fear from labor is much worse than thoughtless" for me to get the idea that there really are limits to the way a person can treat you. I grew up thinking a person, any person, can treat you any way he wants, and you just have to make the best of it.

I have this blind spot. I still have trouble seeing when someone is being extreme or inappropriate. I've learned that I have an almost infinite tolerance for abuse. I always think, "I can take this." Never mind that it's more than 95 percent of what the human race could or should take. I can always bear it. I drive myself to incredible feats— like going to school 10 hours a day, making time for my child, doing three hours of homework each night, driving 90 miles a day to get him to day-care, me to school, me to the research facility, back to day-care, back the 35 miles to get home. I have to get up at 5:00 a.m. and can't get to bed till 11:00 and I'm tired and strung out but I still get mad at myself and feel guilty if I snap at my child or don't give him all the time he wants from me or don't eat perfectly. No matter how much I'm required to do, I expect to do all of it perfectly.

I expect myself to handle everything without it taking any toll on me. I get mad at myself for feeling tired. I don't recognize my own self-abuse. I don't recognize the abuse I receive because of my own impossible expectations. I'm like a coal miner solely responsible for excavating 10 tons of coal in a week with a teaspoon who says, "That's my job? All right. I'll do it."

I'm used to the feeling of plodding on till the current trial is survived.

We Are Not Born to Be Victims

Inability to distinguish extreme or inappropriate behavior, excessive tolerance for abuse, impossible expectations of self-perfection, inability to defend oneself—these are infallible symptoms of severe childhood abuse.

If a child learns that her only permitted response to abuse is to survive it, how, as an adult, can she magically know that defense is permissible?

Unfortunately, many of us have been in situations where we've been overpowered physically, where someone has used violence or power to take from us. We are not responsible for that harm. An unfortunate consequence of such violence or abuse of power is that we sometimes believe we are born to be victims. We let others commit even nonviolent offenses against us because we've lost the sense (or maybe we never had it to begin with) that we have the right to defend our boundaries.

Why do I say this sense is lost? After you read more of Essie's story you might argue that never in her life did she believe she didn't have to take abuse. I'd have to agree. Some children are so neglected or stifled that they learn to be careful and watchful before they can talk. These early learnings affect our view of the world for the rest of our lives unless careful therapy roots out the problem and heals it.

Even babies, however, can communicate discomfort, and small children, when frightened, draw back or say "No." That first "no," that first drawing back, may be the child's last, but it is an honest defense. If the child is abused for his natural response, he quickly learns to squelch it. We are naturally inclined to defend ourselves from harm and we must be frightened into accepting harm. If, as children, we learn to accept harm, as adults we see harm to ourselves as the way of the world. It's the way things are. We bear it and go on anyway.

Empowerment

My message to you is one of empowerment. If your physical and sexual boundaries have been violated in the past, you were a victim then, but you do not have to be a victim any longer. As of this moment, know that you have the right to determine how your body is treated. Even a light touch can be removed if you don't want it. But how?

Take his hand off your shoulder and say, "No thank you." Move away and say, "I don't like that." Back up and say, "Please ask permission before you touch me." "I like to make the choice about that." "Don't do that again." "Not this year, I have a headache."

We sometimes think we have to be courteous even when the other person is rude. But some people can't hear a tactful message. They need something stronger: "If you don't want a finger replacement, keep your hands to yourself." "Touch me again and I'll scream." "If you keep that up, I'll embarrass you in front of everybody." "I think I'll give your wife a call. She'd be interested to know what you're up to."

When you protect yourself from even mild physical violation, a powerful message is sent through your body. I am me! I am strong! I am valuable! I can keep myself safe. When you protect yourself, you empower yourself.

The following exercises give you practice identifying and stopping subtle violations of your physical boundaries. When you mentally excuse someone of even minor intrusiveness, you continue to give yourself the message that your instincts must be sacrificed even for someone who is boorish and unworthy of what he takes from you. The thief wins and you, despite your goodness, lose.

Learning how to win even these seemingly insignificant contests prepares you to protect yourself from the varsity challenges. The strange thing about being taught to be a victim is that our status is somehow communicated to the persecutors. Someone who's looking to harm someone can pick the victim out of a crowd.

The more you stop yourself from being used, the less you broadcast yourself as a victim. Like a wolf who stalks the weak elk in the herd, exploiters will pass you over if you seem strong and feisty. By learning to protect yourself, you lessen the incidences of being threatened.

Protecting Your Safety Zone

Exercise 4.1

1. Today, notice what physical distance feels comfortable as you interact with people.
2. If someone you don't trust stands too close to you, move to a distance that feels safer. If the person continues to close that distance, move so that something is between the two of you. If nothing is available, put out your arm and say, "Stop. I want you to stay where you are." If the person tries to talk you out of this or asks you to explain yourself, shake your head. You do not have to explain this.
3. Talk to a friend about what you learned.

Saving Your Skin

Exercise 4.2

1. Today and tomorrow, notice when you are touched.
2. Ask yourself, do you want to be touched in that way by that person?
3. Stop the touching if you don't want it.
4. Talk to a friend about what you experienced.

CHAPTER FIVE

YOUR EMOTIONAL BOUNDARIES

Essie's Story

When my therapist asked me to draw my family tree, I asked her, "Which one?" First my mom was married to my dad. Then they divorced. Then Mom married Craig, who had a son and a daughter. My dad married Eve, and they had a daughter. Then he divorced Eve and married Sue and a few years after that divorced Sue and married Nancy. Nancy already had a daughter.

I mostly grew up with Mom and Craig. When I was eleven or twelve, I begged Dad to let me live with him, but he said no. And he said if I said anything about it to Mom, she might not let me see him at all. Also, my mom said she'd kill herself if I left her.

I was four when Mom married Craig. His son, Lew, was in high school. His orbit was so different, I barely knew him. Jackie, his daughter, was eight then. She was my nemesis. When I think about my childhood I just remember it as numberless events in which Jackie hurt me. I'd be sitting on the floor and she'd step on my fingers. I'd be playing with a doll and she'd take it away. She told me she was the most important child, that she was pretty and I was ugly and fat. That she was smart and I didn't know anything. I'd be reading a library book and she'd hit me in the head.

I never tried to tell my mom what it was like, because I knew she wasn't stable. I was worried about her welfare and didn't want to give her anything else to handle. She had enough pain and sadness.

She only talked to me about her worries and concerns. She never asked me about what mattered to me. She seemed unaware of me except in terms of what I could give her.

Mom's first concern was the house. She was always doing housework. We were always to be careful not to mess it up or get anything dirty.

I learned very early not to talk to my mother about anything because she would cry and I'd feel responsible. I'd feel guilty for bothering her and would end up comforting her rather than getting any help.

I can't remember ever being held or her being affectionate with me, except when she was upset and needed a hug. When she hugged me then she clutched me as if I were saving her. I hate it when she hugs me that way now.

Also, I learned a big lesson about not telling her things because of what happened when my dad took me to visit my grandmother. Mom and my grandmother (her mother) didn't get along at all and didn't talk to each other. My grandmother wanted desperately to see me, but Mom wouldn't let me see her. So my grandmother kept calling my father and pleading with him to bring me to see her. He did. I was very excited about it. I was about 7. I didn't know it was supposed to be a secret so I told my mom. She was so upset that she wouldn't let me see my dad for years and wouldn't let me stay all night at his house till I was about 13. From then on, I never told my mom anything important.

Those years I couldn't see him were horrible for me because visiting my dad was the best thing in my life. With him I was safe from being hurt. Also, he noticed me. He looked at me. He talked to me. He didn't use me.

I became very attached to his wives, trying to bond with someone, I guess. Also, I talked to my dad through them.

Dad hated for me to cry. He'd clam up and not talk if I cried, so I learned to be happy and chatty when I was with him. I learned to be entertaining. He didn't want to know about troubles.

When he gave me gifts, though, it was an agony. When Jackie found out she'd have a fit. She would hurt me worse than usual and tear up or ruin whatever I'd gotten.

It got so I dreaded Christmas or my birthday. Jackie would lie in wait to see what my dad had given me. It didn't do any good if I tried to hide it or act like it wasn't very important to me. It didn't even matter that Dad usually got a present for Jackie at Christmastime. She'd still take what I had or mess it up.

That's when I must have started making excuses for people. I still can't think someone is being deliberately mean. I can excuse anything by thinking, he didn't mean to do it, he's just upset. When Hal hit me, I never thought of him as just a mean person. I used to tell myself that Jackie did these things because Mom and I had invaded her house when Mom got married, so maybe I deserved it.

I think I believed I wasn't worth much. That's why the house was so important to Mom and that's why she missed what Jackie was doing to me. I decided I wasn't worth being noticed by Mom and I was better off not being noticed by Jackie.

Whenever I was home I made myself melt into the woodwork. I didn't want to be seen as special in any way at all. I didn't want to have anything special. I just wanted to be left alone.

As I got older, Mom leaned on me a lot. She always had a lot of worries. She worried about money and about Craig never being home and about her weight. Craig divorced her after I left home and whenever I saw her she was depressed and needing to talk about it.

She'd come to my apartment and see that we didn't have something and next time she'd bring it. Every time she came she brought food or a set of dishes or some money. Whatever she brought I always needed desperately. But then she'd talk and talk about her troubles. I'd be washing clothes, running up and down two flights to the machines in the basement, or fixing dinner or bathing the baby and she'd sit down and talk. I felt like I had to have an answer for her, just like when I was a kid. I felt responsible for helping her life get better.

When I was having trouble with Hal I desperately needed support and wished I could have told her but I didn't want her to know how things really were.

It's funny when I have a birthday now. I want so much for someone to notice and to recognize me, yet if I get a gift, I can't stand it. I know I'll have to pay for whatever I get and the price has always been too high.

Jenny's Story

[Author's Note: As Jenny tells her story, she will reveal cognitive and reasoning abilities that developed at a very young age. Jenny has a brilliant mind and was probably a child prodigy. As you read her story, keep in mind that she has exceptional capacities that as a child were continually misunderstood and thwarted.]

I have really clear memories of my childhood. I remember incidents and thoughts and feelings from when I was a year and a half old. That's when my brother was born and my life stopped. It's only since I've been in therapy that it's started again.

When I was less than two, I remember sitting on a quilt next to this baby and being told by my mother, "Take care of your brother." As young as I was, I remember thinking, I don't know how to do this, I'm not big enough.

I probably remember this incident so clearly because it turned out to be my job description. From then on, it was clear that my brother was the important child in the family. I was the Cinderella, with no fairy godmother.

When I was four and he was two and a half, he pushed me down the stairs. I curled up at the bottom and cried. When Mom asked why I was making such a fuss and I told her, she said Chuck wouldn't do that. I must have slipped.

When I was playing with something that Chuck wanted, sometimes he'd take it. I'd take it back, then he'd protest and fight me for it, crying loudly if he couldn't get it. Whenever he cried, Mother came running. She didn't like being interrupted and she blamed me for it. "What did you do to him?" she snapped.

"Nothing. He took my toy and I took it back."

"Give it to him. You can play with something else."

I ended up feeling so wrong and misunderstood when these things happened.

I was content just doing something by myself, playing or reading or watching the birds. Often at these times, Chuck would walk up and hit me. I hated being hit and I'd push him away so he wouldn't do it again. He yelled, Mom came, and it was my fault that he cried. He was never wrong.

I learned that if I defended myself against him, he'd get Mom's attention and I'd be in trouble. If I just took what he did, at least Mom wouldn't yell at me.

No matter what happened, she always saw me as the one at fault. After all, I was still in charge of him. I wasn't really supposed to be playing anyway. I was supposed to be taking care of him, giving him things to do, watching over him. My job was to mother Chuck.

But then my mom was always saying things like, "You don't want to get married. Being a wife is hell. Don't ever be a mother, it's the worst mistake you can make."

In fourth grade, I was the angel in the Christmas play. I was so excited. It was the first time I'd been chosen to do something special. I got to wear this beautiful white robe and wings. It matched my dream about having wings so I could fly away and find a nicer family.

It's all I talked about for weeks, but when I asked Mom and Dad if they were coming, Dad never answered and Mom said only probably. In my enthusiasm, I missed the lack of theirs.

I felt like an angel as I was getting dressed for the play. I felt beautiful in my gown and wings. The mother who dressed me said I was pretty. When I was ready, I ran up the back of the stage and peeked through the curtain. Lots of parents had already gathered but I didn't see mine.

I was so sure they'd be there. After the play started and they still weren't there, I thought they were running late or looking for a parking place or that I just couldn't see them in the audience.

At some point the hope drained out of me in one complete emptying. I knew they wouldn't come and that they never would. So I became cynical. I wasn't even mildly surprised when they made a big production out of Chuck being in Little League.

Dad drank a lot. Mom and Dad fought with words and fists. I wasn't even ten when I started planning the life I would have when I left home.

In high school, I scored really high on a battery of tests. When my teachers saw the test scores, they didn't react with encouragement or enthusiasm. I never heard, "Wow, Jenny, you could be good at anything you wanted to do." Their attitude was, "It doesn't matter, Jenny. Women don't amount to much. Pick what you want because it won't make much difference."

When I was taking chemistry in high school, I said to my dad that it was really hard, and to that he said, "If you think that's hard, that's nothing compared to college." He said that to me so much that I became terrified of college. I knew he was trying to tell me I wasn't good enough to handle it. So when I graduated I went to business school.

Eventually I got a job in a bank and took extra night courses so that I would truly understand all the parts of banking. Before long I was a trust officer administering my own accounts. From my first days there, women were always paid less than men. When I said that to my dad, he said, "Of course. Men have families to support."

And I said, "What about Shirley? Her husband died, she has two small children, and one needs an operation. She gets half the pay of men in her position."

"Too bad," he said. "She'll manage somehow."

When I became an officer, the accounts I took on were a mess. To fix them meant exposing the shoddy work of the man who'd had the position before me. I believed in giving good service to my clients so I did what had to be done. It didn't help the way the men saw me. I wasn't a team player who backed up the boys in the club no matter what. My clients liked me though, and I got a lot of new accounts.

The bank was restructured and I was laid off because I didn't have a degree. Because the credentials I'd built up through night courses weren't degree oriented, they didn't count.

At that point, I quit trying. When I left home, I thought if I tried hard and followed the rules I'd have control over my life, but I was wrong. I grew up before women had any say. Everywhere I looked, men had the choices and women were to serve. Having a sense of justice, being conscious of inequities, even just being conscientious —these things counted for nothing.

When I was young, I married a man who turned out to be an alcoholic, so I left him. I had this little piece of property from my father—I'd dreamed of building a house on it—but I had to sell it when I left my husband, just to get enough money to get back home.

Eventually though I did buy a little house. It was the first thing that was mine. I didn't have much money so I furnished it bit by bit with things from garage sales or store closeouts. Then I invited my father, my brother and his wife, and my half-sister from my mother's first marriage over for dinner. I lived only twenty miles from all of them but in twenty-four years my dad visited me three times, my half-sister once (when she wanted to sell me something), and my brother and his wife a few times.

I didn't even know, till I got in therapy, that I was depressed all those years or that I had a reason for being depressed. I just kept trying and not understanding why I was so invisible to everybody. Why didn't I count? Why had I never counted? Because I was female?

They wouldn't come to my house, but I went to theirs—on holidays when it was expected that the whole family would come together. I was always received with a patronizing, "And here's Jenny!" They might just as well have said, "And here's the fifth wheel. Where shall we put it?"

After some therapy, I quit going. I quit trying to pretend I had family in those people.

When Gil came into my life, I was swept away. He was the first man who had ever been kind to me. He was warm, interested, and caring. He supported me and valued my talents. My heart stood up and followed him like a child follows candy.

That he was married was agonizing to me, but I couldn't stop myself. I was violating my deepest values, but I needed what he gave me like a desert needs rain. I lived in this tension for twenty years.

When he became free, we had a new set of problems. I had thought we were very intimate but it was different once we could be with each other every day. I kept looking for him to take me in, to comprehend my deepest inner self, and he seemed to barely hear me. I'd get so angry.

When we had a problem, I wanted to work it out. I'd try to get him to problem-solve, but sometimes he seemed unconscious of me, the problem, and the value in attending to problems. I'd tell him I felt removed from him, that I needed him to listen to me and that I wanted him to tell me what he was feeling. All he could say was, "I feel fine." Then two hours later he'd want to make love.

Hadn't he heard a word I'd said? Did he think I wanted to make love when I felt so unconnected to him? This kind of thing happened all the time. Our affair hadn't shown me how different we were. I guess anyone can offer a sincere ear a couple of hours a week.

For a while it looked as if we were going to part company. We're good companions and he's a pleasure to be with, but feeling unheard kept me mad all the time and him feeling pressured all the time and it looked like that was going to break us apart. We did therapy together and it seemed to get clearer that he wanted to call off our marriage.

Much has changed now. I expect less of him. I'm slowly understanding that he prefers to be less conscious of himself and life. I kept denying this was true of him because I strongly value self-awareness and awareness of relationships. For so long, despite consistent evidence, I couldn't take in that his preference was so different than mine. I kept trying to make him conscious. I thought if I showed him what was missing, he'd grasp it eagerly. I see now that he doesn't want to grasp it. He prefers floating along in a cloud of simple routine and superficial contact.

All that's changed now. We're easy with each other now. We are closer. What made the difference? I don't know. Nothing dramatic happened.

I kept going to therapy and working hard there and things changed. Each week so much was revealed to me. Gradually I seemed to have myself again, the self that was lost before I was two.

I never saw, for example, that I was a neglected child or that I lived with a lot of abuse. I never saw how programmed I was to not have a life of my own. My purpose in life was to take care of

Chuck. I was programmed to not be a mother, both because I was burned out from mothering Chuck and because of the way Mom downgraded motherhood.

I was discouraged from choosing a career I might like or from getting an advanced education. Being a woman, nothing I did would count. I didn't even have a husband of my own. I borrowed someone else's.

For most of my life I didn't feel anger at my mother, but I lived it out by constantly struggling between doing what she taught and not doing what she taught.

Whatever she told me to do I rebelled against. A woman was supposed to keep a neat house. After I left the bank and quit trying, I couldn't clean my house to save my soul. I hated seeing the piles grow, but I couldn't make myself pick things up. Yet I wanted it to be neat so it would be pleasant to live in. For years I struggled over this, never being comfortable in my house yet paralyzed when I tried to straighten it.

I lived out this kind of struggle in so many ways it was practically all my life consisted of. It exhausted me. I never knew if I liked something because it was what I truly wanted or if I liked it because Mother would have hated it. Yet every choice against her filled me with guilt. In every way I saw myself a failure.

Since therapy I have more energy. As I lose my shackles, I'm able to make choices. I can live in moderation instead of in reaction to my mother, either in the one extreme of what she would approve of or in the other of what she would hate. I'm doing things for my own reasons now.

I wanted so desperately for Gil to hear me because I couldn't hear myself. I wanted someone to draw me out of the place I'd been buried.

Maybe things are so much better between us because now I can take care of myself. Every week, I'm emerging. I'm clearer, freer. I have a me. I don't need him to do that now. I can do it. I trust myself. I believe in myself.

I lived under a cloud for so many years, sometimes I get scared that it will come back, that it's this happiness that's temporary. But I am believing more and more that this is the real me and the sad, hopeless person I used to be won't visit me for very long ever again. Mostly I believe that this process I'm in can continue to be trusted.

The longer I work, the more that other self recedes like a station left behind a departing train.

Our Boundaries, Our Selves

Essie and Jenny are two bright, perceptive women who might easily have been lost to us. I don't mean they might have died, although people have taken their lives or had their lives taken in less extreme circumstances. What I mean is that we as a people might have been cheated of the special awareness and talents these incredible, powerful women have to offer.

Advancements in psychotherapy and a growing understanding of the recovery process have returned to the world these and many other men and women whose selves were stolen by abusive or neglectful childhoods.

The development of emotional boundaries and the development of self go hand in hand. Weak boundaries equal a weak self-image; a healthy self-image equals healthy boundaries. Boundaries without a self would be like a punctured balloon. It collapses when nothing is inside. A self without boundaries is like air without a balloon, shapeless, formless, diffused.

Jenny and Essie were both abused by siblings. The abuse progressed because their parents were emotionally absent. Abuse flourishes in an atmosphere of neglect.

Essie survived her stepsister's abuse, her mother's neglect, and her father's unconsciousness in a subtle way that went unnoticed by her absent parents. She gave herself up. By deliberately withdrawing from being special she made herself invisible. She didn't want to stand out. So she took her selfness off like a dangerous garment. Then because she felt safe only with her father, and so could not risk losing his necessary visits, she created a false self that would entertain him.

Neither Essie nor Jenny were allowed a sense of ownership over their own things. Essie's sister broke anything she treasured. Jenny was supposed to share all that was hers with Chuck. Both grew up feeling that nothing of theirs was safe and exclusively theirs. They learned to expect little.

The Right to Have a Self

Throughout her childhood Jenny received consistent messages: She was not allowed her life for its own sake. She lived only to serve her brother. Jenny, however, was born with a very clear sense of self. At an early age she had strong values and spontaneous contact with her feelings. Most of us have no other frame of reference than that which we get from our parents, but Jenny had an inner voice that told her something was wrong with the way she was being treated.

That so much native strength was defeated demonstrates the power a dysfunctional family can have. The disease of the parents defeated the health of the child. Jenny had drummed out of her her right to have a self. But through years of oppression, a spark in Jenny remained alive. This spark, this powerful need to become herself, got Jenny into therapy and kept her devoted to the process until that inner spark could burst into flame.

Both Jenny and Essie were robbed of their individuality. They were not allowed boundaries. They were not protected so that they could keep a self. Thousands of people grow up in this condition— walking shells whose inner self has been squashed or destroyed— shells filled with some other person's dreams or values or filled with hate and anger or drugs or a drive to gather lots of things, anything to not feel so empty.

Building Up and Tearing Down

Emotional boundaries define the self. Assaults to boundaries threaten the self. One's unique self is composed of a complex of ideas, feelings, values, wishes, and perspectives that are duplicated by no other. Emotional boundaries protect this complex.

What strengthens emotional boundaries? The right to say no. The freedom to say yes. Respect for feelings. Support for our personal process. Acceptance of differences. Enhancement of our uniqueness. Permission for expression.

What harms emotional boundaries? Ridicule. Contempt. Derision. Sarcasm. Mockery. Scorn. Belittling feelings. Stifling communication. Insistence on conformity. Arbitrariness. The need to overpower. Heavy judgments. Any kind of abuse. Abandonment. Threat. Insecurity.

On one end of the scale is the serious abuse and neglect reported in a number of the stories in this book. But what about some milder examples of ways we ruff up our emotional boundaries?

Being Someone You're Not

Think of the effect it has to pretend you're different than you really are. Being someone you're not lets alien behavior and attitudes enter your boundary and replace your true self. When we do this a lot, we begin to feel strange to ourselves. We can lose touch with our true selves and not know what we really want and need.

A clean, clear boundary preserves your individuality, your youness. You are an individual, set apart, different, unique. Your history, experiences, personality, interests, dislikes, preferences, perceptions, values, priorities, skills—this unique combination defines you as separate from others.

When you share yourself honestly, when you reveal your own thoughts and reactions, you define yourself emotionally both to yourself and to others. When you pretend to take on another's views, when you conceal your conflicting opinion, you obscure your boundaries for yourself and for others.

If you smile at a joke you find offensive, how does it feel? If you pretend to hold a political opinion contrary to your real views, what happens inside you? Denying your true self feels bad. But sometimes we feel we have to do it, usually when our survival is in some way threatened.

Has this ever happened to you? Bill Mason went to lunch with other folks from the office. They all were adamantly against the new recycling law. Bill thought the law a good one. He kept quiet because he wanted to belong to the group. His economic survival felt tied to the acceptance of the group.

Here are some other ways you can deny your true self and weaken your emotional boundaries:

- Pretending to agree when you disagree: "I love that color." (You really hate that color.)
- Concealing your true feelings: "I wasn't hurt." (You were terribly hurt.)
- Going along with an activity that you really don't want to do and never stating your preference: "That movie is fine with me." (You'd rather take a walk.)
- Declining to join an activity you really want to do: "No thanks, you guys go ahead." (You're aching to belong.)
- Pushing yourself beyond your limits
- Working too hard
- Working too long
- Doing too much for others
- Not resting when tired

- Ignoring your needs
- Not eating regular, healthy meals
- Insufficient sleep
- Too little or too much alone time
- Too much or too little exercise
- Insufficient contact with people who truly care about you
- Insufficient or too many leisure activities
- Using chemicals to avoid yourself: nicotine, alcohol, caffeine, sugar, pills, drugs
- Using compulsions to avoid yourself: eating, starving, exercise, work, shopping, spending, TV, sex, games, sports—all can be done compulsively

If you are painfully familiar with these examples, I'll bet a quarter that you learned to sacrifice your true opinions to survive some unhealthiness in your original family.

Denying Ourselves Feels Safer

The harm we received as children often sets us up for continued harm as adults. If, as children, we had to deny our true thoughts or feelings to be safe, as adults we are likely to continue to deny what's true for us. Telling the truth feels very unsafe, a threat to survival.

What a dilemma. Denying ourselves feels safer, but it obscures our sense of who we are. The safe route, however, violates an emotional boundary.

What's the way out of the dilemma? If boundary development was severely harmed when you were a child, therapy may be the most efficient route. When we don't work ourselves free of the issues that got started when we were children, we are destined to relive them again and again. "Children who suffer trauma to core self and identity . . . ," writes Jane Middleton-Moz, "work toward resolution of that trauma and completion of development in adult life through repetition of the struggle with authority figures, in intimate relationships, through their own children or in therapy."[3]

Either we wrestle with these issues endlessly with bosses, friends, spouses, co-workers, and children, or we get professional help that

---

[3] Jane Middleton-Moz, Children of Trauma, (Florida: Health Communications, 1989), p. 64.

shows us how to build boundaries and stay safe as well.

What else can you do to reinforce your sense of self and your emotional boundaries? We'll be getting to that in Chapter Nine.

Checking Fences

Exercise 5.1

Equipment: 25–30 pennies, an outfit with at least one pocket

Part 1.
1. Keep the pennies in your pocket or in a pile on your desk or in a bag close at hand. This is the bank.
2. Today and tomorrow, every time you reinforce your true self by stating your true feeling or opinion or by making a healthy choice for yourself, give yourself a penny.
3. Tomorrow night, count your pennies. Put the bank away.

Part 2.
1. On the third and fourth day from today, carry the pennies you earned in your pocket.
2. Every time you deny yourself by misrepresenting your true thoughts or feelings or by making harmful choices, give a penny away. If you run out of pennies, borrow some nickels from your regular funds and pay those to the bank.
3. At the end of the fourth day, count the pennies that are yours. Are you out of pennies? Count the nickels in the bank. Did you deny yourself more than you gave yourself?
4. Discuss what you learned with a true friend.

Inner Consequences

Exercise 5.2

Part 1.
1. Focus on an incident in which you denied your true self. Think about it. Feel about it.
2. Write out the incident. Describe each way you denied yourself and how that felt. Picture how you felt when the incident was over. Picture your boundaries at that moment. Were your bounda-

ries clear to you? Did you have a clear sense of yourself? Were your boundaries fuzzy?

Part 2.
1. Focus on an incident in which you asserted your true self. Think about it. Feel about it.
2. Write out the incident. Describe each way you asserted your true self and how that felt. Picture how you felt when the incident was over. Picture your boundaries at that moment. Were your boundaries clearer to you? Did you have a more distinct sense of yourself? Were your boundaries reinforced?
3. Read your writings to a trusted friend.

CHAPTER SIX

ASSORTED BOUNDARIES

Dogs Come When They're Called

Boundaries come in many varieties. They can be rigid, flexible, permeable, or impermeable. They can be set at a great distance or be very close.

If we agree with writer Mary Bly, dogs and cats can illustrate these differences. "Dogs," she writes, "come when they're called; cats take a message and get back to you."

My dog wants to be as close as possible to me. The great tragedy of her life is that she wants more than anything in the world to be a lap dog, but at 50 pounds can't. She's constantly aware of me and will even wake from a sleep to go with me. Her family is the center of her life. Her boundaries are set very close. She expects other animals to have the same close boundaries and thus gets in trouble regularly with one of our cats.

Cats Take a Message and Get Back to You

The cats have very distinct boundaries. For the most part, they do only what they want. They occasionally want to be close, but they determine how close and when. After being held for a while, they've had enough. They get up and go to the other end of the couch or to some other soft place to rest. They are aware when I stand up, leave, or enter, but they do not stop what they're doing. If I walk into the room, one eye may open, but then the cat nap continues. Their boundaries are set farther than the dog's and their boundaries are less flexible.

One of the cats, Princess, was raised by the dog. When she was a kitten, Fluff licked and nosed her all the time, sometimes licking so hard that she pushed Princess to the ground or into a wall. Now an adult cat, Princess will let Fluff do what she'd tolerate from no other creature, man nor beast. She'll strut into the room and Fluff will run up to her and lick her vigorously. Her big tongue turns Princess into a soggy mop. But the cat tolerates it, emerging like an unkempt sailor. With her surrogate mother, Princess' boundaries are flexible.

That's My Business

Boundaries can be so close that you are nose to nose with everyone you meet. If you think you have to answer any question put to you, if you think your thoughts and feelings should be revealed to anyone, your boundaries are too close.

You have a right to privacy. You choose what thoughts and feelings you want to share with whom. No one has a right to information you want to keep to yourself. If someone asks an intrusive question, you don't have to pay the penalty for her lack of sensitivity.

Some answers to a thoughtless question are: "I don't feel like talking about it." "I want to keep that to myself." "That's my business." "I'm surprised you think you have a right to that information." "Whoops! That's private."

Leaky Parents

Parents with too close and too leaky boundaries can burden their children with inappropriate information. A child exposed to adult problems thinks she's supposed to have the maturity to handle them and worries that the parent needs more of her than she can give. Such children grow up feeling inadequate and too responsible.

Absorbent Mates

A mate with boundaries set too close can be very vulnerable to her spouse's mood changes. Like a sponge, she absorbs every frown, every tightened jaw, and feels responsible for it. She may take on responsibility that isn't hers. She may do too much for her mate, take over jobs that aren't her province.

In contrast, boundaries can be set too far away. A person can set fences at a great distance from her inner self. When this is the case, even an appropriate, friendly gesture can be seen as intrusive. Such a person is isolated. She'll have trouble making friends, difficulty expressing confidences even to safe people, and live in loneliness.

Distant Boundaries Equal Neglect

When a parent has boundaries that are too wide, the child experiences the abuse of too much distance, neglect, insufficient affection and healthy touching, abandonment, and the fear that comes from not feeling connected to the caregiver in power. The parent's distance may prevent her from bonding with her child. Children sense when a parent isn't bonded and it's a frightening loneliness when the bond is one-way, only child to parent. Parental distance can also prevent the child from bonding with the parent. Such a child may always find it difficult to bond with another. She may follow her parent's example and set distant boundaries.

A mate with boundaries set at a distance from his inner self may have difficulty connecting with his spouse. He may have poor contact with his own feelings and be unable to communicate them. He may interpret affection as intrusive, interest as prying. He may feel easily smothered.

Close and Distant

A parent can be too close and too distant. She can invade a child's space by wanting to know all his secrets, by constantly demanding he think and be a certain way, yet still be emotionally unavailable to the child. A parent may require a child to attend to her every want and need, to be her constant emotional support while she remains blind to his needs.

Of course, a person with very close boundaries can marry someone with very distant boundaries. It happens all the time. Terry has such close boundaries, she's unprotected; Chad has such distant boundaries he can't connect. This causes constant tension in the relationship. So sometimes Terry gives up her boundaries; other times she sets them even closer—in an attempt to demonstrate the feeling process to Chad or to entice him to match her openness. Chad, however, often finds this distasteful and draws back even further. The power struggle between her efforts to draw him closer and his efforts to resist being drawn are the central issue in the relationship.

Estranged from Life

When boundaries are very rigid, new ideas or experiences can't get in. A person who has very rigid boundaries may be difficult to bond with. Such a person has a narrow perspective on life, sees things one way, and can't discuss matters that lie outside his field of vision.

Fred (in Chapter Two) denied the existence of feelings. Remember, he had two remote parents, both of whom were limited in their ability to connect with him. Their lack of connection prevented his feelings from being drawn to the surface, and if any feelings did emerge, they were overwhelming. So as an adult, in situations so extreme Fred could not avoid feeling—like his wife walking out—his grief would burst out uncontrollably. The pain of this, however, in contrast to his usual controlled existence, was so intolerable that he'd submerge it as quickly as possible. He never got accustomed to feeling. He never had a chance to stay with feelings long enough to learn they would abate on their own given enough warm attention.

Fred not only controlled his pain, having fun did not come easy to him, nor did being open to the emotions around a happy event. His face had the same expression when he was addressing a jury as it did on a picnic. In fact he often appeared to have more passion in the courtroom, but this was put on to prove his case. He used the appearance of feeling when it served his purposes.

His wife complained that he would not accept feelings as valid reasons for behavior. If she said she was tired of cooking, he insisted she was being unreasonable. He wouldn't consider boredom or lack of interest to be legitimate reasons and would use all of his debating skills to defeat her statements. They once argued for three hours because she didn't want to cook supper.

Fred was so cut off from his feelings that he responded to his wife like a stone. He barely acknowledged her personal triumphs and when she expressed worry, he'd grimace in disdain. His boundaries were so rigid and impermeable that he couldn't join with others in ordinary human experience.

Too Flexible Boundaries

In contrast, one's boundaries can be so flexible that they can't hold a shape. At a neighborhood party, Eva agreed with one woman that the summer had been so hot that she'd hardly moved outside the house. Fifteen minutes later she agreed with someone else that this year the summer had been much more bearable.

Eva was a chameleon. She responded to whatever was the latest demand. If the phone rang when she was on her way out the door to take the kids to school, she'd talk as long as the caller wanted until the kids got more demanding than the caller.

A person whose boundaries are too flexible may feel overwhelmed with life. Each new demand distracts him. He has difficulty setting priorities and following them. He gets started on one thing only to get sidetracked by something else. He may appear disorganized.

A too-flexible parent deprives children of the sense of security that comes from having a specific schedule, clear limits, and definite standards. Such a parent isn't able to protect her own needs and may raise selfish children who never learn to respect the needs of another. A parent who can't set priorities, who is, for example, perpetually late, can make a child feel unimportant and abandoned. Since he can't make priorities, he can't make the child a priority.

These are extreme examples. The same parent may be too rigid in some ways, too flexible in others, and just right in other ways. A parent who is too flexible, however, can be manipulated by his children, which gives them too much power. Children need limits and structure.

A partner whose boundaries are too flexible can be irritating at the least, and untrustworthy at the extreme. An inability to set limits can lead, for one thing, to inappropriate affection outside the relationship.

A person whose boundaries are too flexible may not even be able to choose a partner or spouse. She may feel she has to respond to whomever needs her and thus marry someone simply because he asked, not because she considered her own preference.

Too flexible boundaries can be a source of irritation in a marriage. A wife may become irritated with her husband's disorder. He may forget to get tickets because his agenda shifted when he saw the shoe-shine machine.

Rubbery boundaries can hurt a marriage. She may let men get too close at parties, permit touching or affection that violates her vow of fidelity. He may lose trust in her because she's so responsive to others.

Where Do You Stop and I Begin?

Boundaries that are too permeable lead to enmeshment. When two people are enmeshed, they are so blended together neither can be very sure where he or she stops and the other begins. If a mother cannot let her daughter individuate, the mother will perceive the daughter's experiences as happening to her.

Sue considered her mother to be her best friend. None of her teen friends had a mother who joined in the way her mom did. They had matching outfits and listened to the same music. Sue's mother learned the dances Sue learned and went to all the games. One day, however, Sue let a friend cut her hair. They spiked it. "How dare you walk around looking like that," said her mother. "What will people think of me?"

When a parent's identity becomes immersed in the child's, both lose. The child has difficulty developing a sense of self. The parent is escaping the tasks of her actual age.

Parents who've focused on survival, who've never had a childhood, are especially vulnerable to this. Now they want to go back and have the fun they missed as kids. Unfortunately, an unlived childhood cannot be lived vicariously. If you missed something as a kid, you have to work it out yourself, not through someone else.

A child who grows enmeshed with a parent is likely to enmesh with a mate. Such a wife will take on her husband's attitudes, interests, and goals as if they were her own. She sees not with her own perspective but with his.

Some signs of enmeshment are speaking for the other, answering for the other, and responding to an event as the other would. It's as if one carries the other around within one's own mind and body.

Mix or Match

People from dysfunctional families can have a hodgepodge of boundaries. A husband's boundaries can be too permeable with the guys and too rigid with his family. A wife's boundaries may be too flexible when she's overeating and too rigid when she's in withdrawal from sugar. The possibilities for confusion are endless.

So what's the goal of a person who wants to be healthy? To form boundaries that have some flexibility and some definite limits, boundaries that move appropriately in response to situations—out for strangers, in for intimates. Boundaries should be distinct enough to preserve our individuality yet open enough to admit new ideas and perspectives. They should be firm enough to keep our values and priorities clear, open enough to communicate our priorities to the right people, yet closed enough to withstand assault from the thoughtless and the mean.

Boundary Conditions Are Crucial

"Everything in the universe consists of something organized surrounded by a boundary . . ." writes Richard Rhodes, paraphrasing British-born metallurgist Cyril Stanley Smith. Smith, says Rhodes, "does the basics better than anyone else I know [and] one of the basics he likes to think about is boundaries."

According to Smith, "the conditions of the boundary," Rhodes continues, "determine whether or not the organism inside will thrive. If its boundary is too rigid and impermeable, the organism can't feed or breathe or excrete wastes—can't communicate effectively with the rest of the universe. If its boundary is too porous, it can't sufficiently isolate itself from the rest of the universe to function—it loses its identity. With amoebas and human beings, with stars and nation-states, boundary conditions are crucial."[4]

The rigid, impermeable boundaries created by the Berlin Wall and symbolized by the Iron Curtain controlled and shaped the cultures they enclosed. Today, however, now that the Wall has fallen and the Iron Curtain as we've known it is no more, East and West are tentatively embracing. The West, especially, is transforming the East.

From this country's earliest days, immigrants and refugees from every continent have landed on U.S. soil only to give up their boundaries. In their urgency to become Americans, many have willingly disowned the cultures that gave birth to them—or, not so willingly, like African-Americans and Native Americans, had their cultures stripped from them by the people in power. The loss of all of these traditions is a loss to all of us.

Healthy boundaries protect without isolating, contain without imprisoning, and preserve identity while permitting external connections. Good boundaries make good neighbors.

Exposing Enmeshment

Exercise 6.1

See if you can identify the statements which reveal enmeshment.
1. "Joan, we want to take you and Harry to dinner. What's your favorite restaurant?"
   "The Seattle Grill," Joan answers automatically. (The Seattle Grill is Harry's favorite restaurant.)
2. "Joan, how are you feeling today?"
   "Harry has a terrible cold. He was up all night."
3. "How was your vacation?"
   "We loved it."
4. "Here's my other half."
5. "Wash your car. It reflects on me."

---

4 Richard Rhodes, "Beyond the Wall," *Rolling Stone*, March 8, 1990, p. 92.

6. "We spend every minute together. He can't stand to have me out of his sight."
7. "I'm hungry."
   "No, you're not."
8. "You can't wear that. I'd be embarrassed."
9. "I don't like oysters."
   "Yes you do."
10. "We agree on everything."

Answers appear at the end of the chapter.

Detecting Boundary Problems

Exercise 6.2

Identify the boundary problems in the following statements.

R	Too rigid	F	Too flexible
P	Too permeable	C	Too Closed
D	Too Distant	E	Enmeshed

1. "What do you want to do this weekend?"
   "Whatever you want to do."
2. "I'm angry with you."
   "No, you're not."
3. "My husband's work is much more important."
4. "She raises the kids. My job is to make money."
5. "Tommy's just like his dad."
6. "I'm sad."
   "I'll show you what sad is."
7. "You must never raise your voice at your sister."
8. "Never talk to your father when he's reading the paper."
9. "Isn't it cute? The twins still dress alike."
10. "I'm a veterinarian and our children will be veterinarians."

Experiencing Walls

Exercise 6.3

Equipment: 25–30 feet of twine per person, a timer, one piece of net or screen or an open-weave fabric for every two people

With a friend or in a recovery or therapy group, experience the following types of boundaries.

Rigid Boundaries

First, you and your partner put your twine on the floor in the shape of a square. Neither square should touch. Then stand in the middle of your squares and discuss one of the following topics for five minutes. One of you may only make statements of feeling; the other, only statements of fact and opinion. When you're finished, discuss how that felt and how it reminded you of your family.

Topics
• Abortion
  Sample exchange on abortion:
  OPINION: "I think a woman should have control over her own body."
  FEELING: "I cried when my daughter aborted her baby."
• The present state of the legal system (for example: criminal rights versus victim rights)
• The latest government scandal
• Gun control (for example: waiting period for handguns versus open sales)
• Animal rights (for example: using animals for research)

Flexible Boundaries
1. Make a circle with your twine but shake your wrist so that the circle is squiggly. Now your partner also makes a squiggly circle, with a portion of her twine overlapping yours.
2. Stand in the middle of your circles. Discuss one of the above topics. Agree with everything your partner says.

Enmeshment
1. Move your circles so that they overlap considerably. Stand in the middle of your circles. Talk about your uniqueness.
2. Move your circles so that they are on top of each other. Stand in the middle. Talk about your separateness from others.
3. After ten minutes, move your circles so that the distance feels comfortable. Discuss how the different degrees of closeness felt and how you were reminded of your family.

Answers. Exercise 6.1 All are indicators of enmeshment.
Exercise 6.2 1. F; 2. E or R; 3. P or F; 4. R; 5. E; 6. R, C, or D;
7. R or D; 8. R or C; 9. E; 10. R & E.

CHAPTER SEVEN

BOUNDARY VIOLATIONS

Closing the Line

A boundary violation is a serious matter. The survivor of the violation bears the brunt of the emotional shock wave created by it, but no one in the immediate system goes unharmed.

A boundary violation is committed when someone knowingly or unknowingly crosses the emotional, physical, spiritual, or sexual limits of another. Boundary violations may be accidental or deliberate. They can be committed maliciously, thoughtlessly, or out of kindness.

Whether a violation is intended or not, whether it is committed out of ignorance or malice, it is still a violation. It still harms. I can't count the number of clients who've protested, "She didn't mean to do it," "He couldn't help it," "She didn't know any better," "That's the way he was brought up."

They defend their parents or partners for reasons that must be explored, but the reality of the violation must not be ignored. Deliberate or not, malevolent or not, boundary violations have consequences, especially for children, consequences that can reach far into the future. For the reverberations to die down, the violation must be identified, the offender named, and the survivor helped to explore and express her feelings and to rebuild the violated boundary.

All Relationships Have Limits

Boundaries tell us that certain behavior is inappropriate in the context of certain relationships. All relationships, even very intimate ones, have limits on what's appropriate. When someone acts inappropriately within the context of the relationship, it often leads to a boundary violation.

Boundary violations can be healed right away if the sufferer tells the intruder that a boundary has been violated and the intruder immediately apologizes or somehow expresses concern about the violation. Note the two parts to this. The one whose limits have been breached must make the offense known and the offender must respect the limit.

Children, of course, can only be aware of their limits if they are allowed to have them. So a parent is responsible for not violating a child's boundaries even though he or she has the power to get away with it.

Your Doctor Is Not Your Peer

Certain roles carry rank or power. Parent, supervisor, boss, owner, teacher, principal, coach, camp counselor, Scout leader, landlord, sergeant, general, therapist, minister, rabbi, guru, counselor, psychiatrist, doctor, attorney, policeman are all roles that carry power.

A supervisor, boss, owner, military officer, teacher, or coach has power because he or she can influence the financial future of the subordinate. The livelihood of the subordinate is in his hands.

Parents, clergy, rabbis, doctors, attorneys, therapists, teachers, and Scout leaders are invested with trust. These positions of leadership involve caring for, advocating for, or teaching those within their charge. They are the designated experts on the slice of life within their bailiwick.

Although we, the people they care for, are not technically subordinate, we entrust these people with authority over life's more critical aspects, authority that enables them to sanction or invalidate us. The leadership and trust we invest in them, however, carries with it a particular responsibility. The development of ethics is a recognition of this responsibility.

A parent has the power to validate or invalidate the worth of his or her child. A therapist is entrusted with his or her clients' deepest secrets. A minister bestows sanctions from the highest power in the universe. The potential for harm is overwhelming.

For a person in such a role, essentially that of a guardian, to cross sexual boundaries is a grave violation. A child, a client, a patient, a follower, a worshiper—all are vulnerable and approaching authority out of need. A sexual action by a guardian is very confusing even to a very strong and healthy individual. For someone vulnerable and in need, such an action can be devastating.

When a parent is sexual toward a child, the violation reverberates for decades. Trust is broken, the child takes on responsibility for the act, sexuality is affected, and the bond is damaged. When a therapist, physician, attorney, or clergyperson is sexual with a client or worshiper, it is also incest. A trust is broken, a bond is perverted.

The person who sought care was used to meet the needs of the caregiver.

More subtle violations occur when the caregiver initiates interaction that is only appropriate among peers. Your doctor is not your peer. Your therapist is not your peer. If you are stripped for someone and that someone is not stripped for you, you are not peers.

How can you tell if someone is a peer? If he knows more about you than you know about him, he is not a peer.

"He's Too Young to Remember What I Did"

The most serious power violation is the sexual boundary violation of a child by a parent or caretaker. Why? When a child's sexual boundaries are violated, the consequences for the child reach far into the future, like a hand that stretches through years to mangle the days and hours of a lifetime.

A family that permits sexual abuse trains children to be victims and predators. Why do I use the word *permit?* Mothers have been known to subtly hand a child over to a father in order to keep him connected to the family. This is an extreme example perhaps, but incest is also permitted when a parent looks the other way, is too busy to know what's really happening to a child, or sustains an atmosphere in which children aren't safe enough to express their feelings.

Families permit abuse for particular, convoluted reasons. Children can be sacrificed for the security, sexual, or emotional needs of the parents.

In Chapter Two, Donna spoke of the sexual violations committed by her father from the time she was four. She is a bright, warm, attractive woman. She told about the years she gave everything of herself to her husband and children. Her childhood abuse prevented her from developing boundaries.

Many of my clients who were abused as children have little sense of boundaries. Sexual violation seems to annihilate emotional, spiritual, and relational boundaries as well. A single sexually exploitative incident in childhood, not necessarily penetration, but inappropriate touching or looking, causes exhaustive damage.

When I hear the phrase "mild sexual abuse," I shudder. Any sexual abuse reverberates. "He's too young to remember what I did." Bodies, apparently, remember everything, even if the mind's recall is hazy. Incidents that occur before the child can talk brand the mind with indelible messages. These messages control the grown human daily until careful, skilled therapy weakens their power.

Attention! Sexual boundary violations have severe, longlasting, widespread consequences. Such violations impair total boundary development.

Children Pick Up on Everything

What is a sexual boundary violation? Inappropriate touching, speaking, or looking that sexually gratifies one person at the expense of the other, who is unwillingly exploited. In the case of a child, this includes inappropriate touching, speaking or looking that gratifies an older person sexually.

Many children are like miniature radar receivers. They pick up on everything. They are highly observant and aware of nuance, implication, a glance. Their interpretations and conclusions stem from five delicate senses. These interpretations can have the force of a bullet.

A father who pleasures in the developing body of his teenager, however subtly, communicates this to the daughter. She knows this is happening. She becomes unsafe in her home. Even if he would never touch her, her safety has been violated.

A mother who toys with the genitalia of an infant, male or female, exploits the child's trust for the sake of her own curiosity. How do children know the difference between touching that promotes hygiene and sexual or exploitative touching? They know.

You know, don't you? One coworker hugs you at Christmas and you feel nourished. Another guy hugs you and you want to send your clothes to the cleaners. How do you know? You just know, right? Children know too.

Exploitation Affects Boundary Development

When a child is sexually violated, a shotgun effect of consequences can result. She can grow up believing her role is to give herself away. She may have no sense of herself. She may believe she is not allowed to set limits with people or that if she does, her limits will always be overpowered. She may get affection confused with sex, using sex to get nurturing or affection or fearing affection will cause sex. She may set boundaries that are so rigid that she won't allow anyone into her life. She may overeat so that fat can provide a wall for her. She may become a frightened person with no inner sense of safety. The possibilities are endless.

These boundary violations can be healed but it takes time and lots of work.

Exploitative Contact Steals

Sexual boundary violations can be committed by anyone in a position of power. Older siblings, neighbors, and relatives are all more powerful than a child. The parent is responsible for seeing that the child is with truly safe people, and for making it easy for the child to talk about anything so that if someone does violate trust, he or she will know it's okay to say so.

Other violations of trust and power occur when a doctor, therapist, clergyperson, or attorney is sexual with a client or patient. Sexual comments, sexual touching, or sexual looking exploit the person in need, who often has handed over authority to the professional. Someone seeking help from a doctor or minister is more vulnerable and less defended than someone parking a car or shopping for broccoli.

If your boss pats you on the fanny or brushes against your breasts, it's a sexual boundary violation. If over the years you've developed a warm, trusting relationship, a hug feels good. You can tell the difference.

No One Owns Your Body

Exploitative contact steals. Nurturing contact fills.

Other power violations include physical and emotional abuse of subordinates. When a father's spanking becomes a beating, it's a violation of the child's physical boundaries. When a boss yells abusively at a technician, it's a violation of an emotional boundary.

Touching that hurts, harms, or degrades is a physical violation. A boss pinching her secretary, a teacher tweaking a student's ear, a coach slapping a player's face—all are committing violations. No matter how exalted a person's position, she does not own someone else's body. We all have the right to limit or deny another's touch.

Violation of emotional boundaries occurs when an authority thinks he has the power to say anything he wants to someone else. A supervisor has no right to remark on your body unless it has a direct connection with job performance. Sexual comments, as I said, are simply out of place. Also inappropriate are comments about body size, height, weight, age, face. "She's a short little thing," sounds harmless enough, but that the boss thinks she has the right to make such a comment is not harmless.

Yelling at a subordinate beyond a quick, normal, healthy expression of anger is a violation. Sarcastic comments are violating. Derogatory, insulting, disparaging remarks violate the emotional boundaries of the recipient.

Such comments imply entitlement. The authority is assuming she is entitled to say anything she wants without regard for the recipient. The following comments are inappropriate:

- A tirade directed at the recipient that goes on and on.
- "You've put on a few pounds, haven't you?"
- "Daughter, dear, it's too bad you can't keep your house as neat as your sister's."
- "Jimmy, you are a stinky boy."
- "Get that list to me or you're fired!"
- "You forgot a pencil? You're a stupid, forgetful slob."

Your Therapist Is Not Your Buddy

Roles carry built-in limits. What is appropriate when your role is mom is inappropriate when your role is boss. A common type of violation occurs when the limits of a role are ignored or forgotten.

Your therapist is not your buddy. Certain therapeutic approaches say it's okay to be friends or even lovers with clients. As a victim of this philosophy I can testify that this confusion of roles leads to confusion of boundaries.

Professional distance between therapist and client gives the client her greatest safety. Friends give and take from each other. A client is safest if the therapist has no expectation of receiving from the client. Friends develop obligations. A client has no obligation to the therapist other than the financial one. A therapy session is strictly for the purpose of advancing the client's emotional growth. The focus is on the client. In a friendship, the focus moves back and forth.

Social contact between therapist and client muddies the boundaries. I used to go to client weddings but now I don't. I am not a buddy. I am also not a parent. My presence in other contexts confuses the fact that I have a special, unique, protected role in her life with specific limitations. Seeing the client in a strictly defined context gives her the widest opening into her own internal processes. It reduces to a minimum the interpersonal anxiety that exists between any two people and therefore increases the intrapersonal awareness that leads the client into her own feelings.

Your Boss Is Not Your Dad

No matter how paternal your boss seems, you are not his priority. A supervisor who invites confidences, who treats you as a peer, or who leans on you for support is violating a boundary.

Your supervisor can never be your therapist. No matter how much he cares, his own job is most important to him. If he has to sacrifice you to keep his position, he'll do it.

Your supervisor is not your peer. He has the power to get you fired. You can't truly be buddies.

You are not your supervisor's therapist. Your supervisor's job is to support you as a worker. It is not your job to help him work out his personal problems. If you become his sympathetic ear, your own loyalty becomes divided. Your energy is diverted from your actual work and a bond is created that causes confusion between your loyalty to yourself and to the company.

Good supervision is quite a lot like good parenting. It allows for safe communication, security in risking, appropriate meeting of needs, attention to role requirements, and support of subordinates. The goal is the maximum and finest development of the worker as expressed in the medium of his work.

All roles have built-in limits. Respecting these limits creates order in relationships. Crossing these limits yields confusion and disorder.

"Your Father Is No Good in Bed"

A special category of emotional violation is called triangulation. This happens when a third inappropriate person is made privy to information that belongs strictly within a relationship.

Triangulation commonly occurs when a parent confides private information about the other parent to a child. "Your father is no good in bed," is inappropriate to say to a child under thirty and questionable for a child over thirty. Children should not be drawn into their parents' private sexual battles.

"Tell your mother I'll get her that check when I'm good and ready." Emotionally charged statements should go directly to the person involved, not through a child. Even though we all know we're not supposed to shoot the messenger, very likely the child will receive the ire that belongs to the father. "Damn! Damn! Damn!" says Mom, and Sally cringes.

Passing on a secret confided by a friend violates her trust. Talking about your issues about one friend with another friend harms three relationships—your relationship with your absent friend, your friend's relationship with your absent friend, and your relationship with the person you're talking to. (Do you think she'll continue trusting you when she catches on that you gossip about people you say you care about?) If you have an issue with Dave, it will not be worked out by talking about it to Don. To work out an issue with Dave, talk to Dave.

Triangulation can occur between adult family members.

Mom: "Do you know what your sister said to me?"

Son: "No, and don't tell me. Whatever it is is between you and her."

Sis: "I hate the way mother dresses."

Me: "Then tell her, it won't do any good telling me."

Sis: "I thought you could talk to her about it. You're so good with words."

Me: "That's not going to work on me. I'm not going to tell her. It's not my issue."

Friend Carol: "Wait till you hear what Tina said."

Friend Helen: "Don't tell me. Tina's my friend. I don't talk about my friends behind their backs."

What do you do if the issue involves addiction or compulsion? What if you suspect that a good friend is back into drinking or over-working? If you are in a Twelve Step program like Overeaters Anonymous or Alcoholics Anonymous, talk to your sponsor. Talk to your therapist. Talk to another recovering person who doesn't know your friend and keep her name confidential. Go to Al-Anon or Codependents Anonymous. People who understand recovery can help you determine your responsibility to your friend and how to act on it.

Murder By Mouth

Gossip, murder by mouth, is a form of triangulation. A third person is being brought into your issues with someone else, no matter how you try to disguise it. You say you're just passing on innocent information? Why, I ask you? Underneath, are you jealous, are you angry, with your absent friend? You'd get more out of looking at your underlying motivations and dealing with these directly.

Are there any exceptions? I can think of one. If you sense that a friend or someone in your workplace is behaving somewhat abnormally and you're trying to check your perceptions with someone else who knows this person, it may be necessary to discuss him with a third party.

Intent is important here. If your intent is to malign him, look at yourself. If your intent is to get clear to protect yourself from him, with the possible outcome of helping him, then talking to someone else who knows him may be the only option you have.

The Constitutional Right to Talk about Your Boss

I'd guess bosses are the victims of gossip more than any other group of people. Subordinates trade information and irritations about their supervisors as if it were a constitutional right. Perhaps it is.

A boss who is open-handed, fair, and approachable by subordinates, and who maintains excellent boundaries between himself and his subordinates, is usually safe from being the brunt of gossip. After all, if workers can tell you their gripes, they don't have to tell their colleagues.

If you're in a supervisory position, here are some of the things you can do to be the headliner of gossip.

Be a corporate Hitler. The guy who makes a big deal out of his power, who abuses his power, will be a hot topic. Workers won't feel safe telling him their true opinions and will be forced to band together to maintain safety and self-esteem.

Use subordinates as confidants. A supervisor who does this will get a backlash one way or another. The subordinate might reveal what she knows to allay the discomfort of her boss' inappropriate behavior. Then the whole staff will know the boss' secrets.

On the other hand, the subordinate might keep the confidence and resent the burden of it. This resentment will affect work somehow. She has more power than she should. She may use it to better her position. She may sabotage the job to get rid of the burden. She may get angry about other problems on the job that deserve not anger but attention.

Supervisors should confide in other supervisors at their same level. But what does one do if he's the single person at his level in the company? He looks up or down but not across? Confide in a therapist, a recovering person, a sponsor, a trusted friend, or someone in a similar position in another company.

Someone with a character disorder or an untreated addiction or compulsion, even a subtle one, can upset the workplace considerably. A supervisor with such a problem can undermine all her subordinates. One's only defense may be to collaborate with another to protect one's job or work. Here's where a strict chain of command works against productivity. The workplace can develop all the roles and craziness of a dysfunctional family.

Triangulation as a Defense

Poor supervision causes gossip to rise. The weak supervisor, the abusive supervisor, the supervisor who steals ideas or takes credit for the work of subordinates will become the focus of attention. Eyes will be on him rather than the work.

The boss who uses his power to get away with sexual violations can be sure his name will be taken in vain. Every woman in the place will soon be on to him and respect for him will drop like a stone.

In these examples, triangulation becomes a defense. Triangulation becomes a way to offset the abuse of power and to get clarity about the wrongs committed.

This kind of triangulation occurs in families where one member is abusing his or her power. Like a poor boss, an abusive parent who is deaf to protest gives the children no choice but to talk about that parent. When a parent refuses to hear the issues of adult children, the children turn either to each other or to outsiders, but both sides lose. The parent loses an opportunity for greater closeness with the child and the adult child must grieve the loss of the sought-for resolution that cannot come about.

It's clear, then, that the issue of triangulation is not clear. Triangulation harms relationships, but we perpetuate it when we abuse power or refuse to listen.

If He Hasn't Changed, He'll Probably Hurt You Again

How can you tell when to approach someone about your issues with him? Answer these questions. Is this person safe? Has this person been abusive or misused important information in the past? If he has been abusive, has he undergone any recovery process since then that would change his ability to respond to you? If he has not entered therapy or recovery, why should his response be any different? If he is still drinking or still unaware of his unhealthy response to you, trusting him with more personal information will probably hurt you.

As much as we want to improve our relationships with our fathers or mothers, if your father, for example, hasn't changed, he'll probably hurt you again. His response is saying that he can't handle more intimacy with you. Repeated efforts on your part won't change this. No matter how much we love someone, they have the choice of holding to their limits.

I have a certain relative I love very much. I've poured my heart out telling of my wish that we might be closer. I've been hurt a hundred times. So I finally got it. No matter how much I want to be closer to my relative, I can't make him take his barrier away. He has a right to keep it. But I can protect myself from being hurt again. I can stop banging my head on his barrier.

Some people do change. In this case, the risk of opening yourself might be worth it. Take a small risk and see what happens. If it turns out well, take another small risk of revealing something about yourself. Take little steps in exposing yourself and stop if it's treated poorly. You've discovered the other person's limit. You'll bear the consequences if you go further.

What's Appropriate?

How can you develop your own sense of what's appropriate?

What's your orientation to the person in question? Do you look up, down, or across? Are you in a receiving or a giving role? Is your role to give or receive support?

If you're looking up to a person for guidance, supervision, or parenting, you are not his peer. If he's your dad, minister, therapist, or boss, you are not required to parent or counsel him.

If you're looking down to a person because she's a child, a client, or a subordinate, she is not your peer. She should not be counseling you. And you should not give her inappropriate personal information.

If you're looking across to a person, she's your peer. You support each other. You confide in each other. Giving goes both ways.

If you're doing peer things with someone you look up or down to, something's wrong. A boundary is being crossed. Talk about it to a peer, a therapist, or someone who is boundary wise.

If you're looking down or up at someone who's a peer, something's wrong. A wife is not a subordinate. A husband is not a boss. Mates are equals. The relationship has lost its footing and needs help.

If it's a part of your job to support your supervisor—if you are a doctor's nurse, a boss' secretary, or in some other kind of position that provides direct support, where's the line? It's appropriate to do tasks that directly influence the effectiveness of her work. Sharpening pencils, making business phone calls, and replenishing supplies all support her professional efforts.

Getting lunch or coffee for her is a gray area. If she's so busy that she can't make the time to get lunch, you're supporting of her work by getting lunch for her. If she has the time and doesn't want to be bothered, you are not supporting her work by getting coffee or lunch for her.

Tasks that are definitely not directly supportive of her work include ordering flowers for her husband, making dinner reservations for her anniversary, getting her uniforms from the cleaners, or picking up her favorite mystery at the book store.

Ask yourself, does this support her work or her life? If it supports her work, it's appropriate.

Do I Stay or Do I Go?

Cleaning up role violations is easiest if both people are working on it, but sometimes you're the only one who understands the problem. If your partner is the one who's unaware, a therapist can be helpful. Since your partner is a peer, teaching or coaching him or her about boundaries violates a boundary. So having a third person coach and teach lets you stay in right relationship to each other.

If your boss is the ignorant party, give him a copy of this book. Perhaps he'd really like to do the right thing if he knew what it was. If addiction or compulsion is involved, however, an intervention that includes his boss may be required before anything changes.

Many of us want health in our relationships, and when we have a choice we choose open, frank communication. But if the other person is simply incapable of acting in a healthy way because of an addiction or personality disorder, we must protect ourselves. Sometimes we need to leave a job to find a healthier work environment. A company or agency that doesn't clean up its act always loses the good people. When the employees get healthy, they leave.

If you are the victim of a boundary violation, present or past, protect yourself. Take yourself out of the situation in which you are being violated as soon as possible. Get support from healthy people so you can leave.

If you've been violated, you've got some grieving to do. Working through the grief will restore the care stolen by the violation. Seek comfort and listening from someone you trust. Investigate the choices you made that got you into that situation and get help so you won't choose it again.

If you attend to your own boundary repair, you'll find yourself in progressively better situations. Instead of being on the defensive, you'll actually have the space and safety to develop, to become more yourself, to live more of the life that's been given to you.

CHAPTER EIGHT

INTIMACY

The Commitment Makes the Difference

Some of what I have to say here will sound hopelessly parental and middle-aged, from a woman who grew up surrounded by flower children and free love. When I was in college, love and sex were an adventure. We disdained the stuffy values of our elders. Today, however, after some twenty years as an adult and a therapist, the misty parental warnings of long ago are echoing in my ears. There is a difference between living together and a witnessed commitment.

Marriage or any committed, espoused relationship offers the greatest opportunity for full emotional and physical intimacy. The commitment makes the difference. Emotional and physical intimacy have the best chance to flourish when you can count on seeing the person tomorrow.

Marriage and partnership also seem to be God's way of offering us a chance to work through our childhood issues. This need, to work out unresolved issues, is what creates the enormous gap between the Disney-like happily-ever-after ideal and the reality of hammering out a relationship amid much toil and tears. ("Marriage is the only war in which you sleep with the enemy." Unknown) Boundary issues comprise a large part of this working-out process.

What We Want

What do we hope to find in marriage? Many of us are looking for support, understanding, companionship, affection, loyalty, financial balance, security, the opportunity for self-expression, and sexual passion and fidelity. Is this so much to ask?

It sounds simple until you add a real person with boundary problems. Imagine finding support, companionship, and affection from Fred. This is a man who's never been helped to acknowledge feelings. His boundaries are so distant you'd need a bus to get from customs to the inner man.

To Communicate, We Need Boundaries

A hundred books on marriage will tell you that communication is the key to a successful relationship. But not just any communication will do. The kind that makes the difference comes from the inner person—important, wispy, hard-to-grasp feelings; tough acknowledgments; needs cloaked in shame—and goes to the other's inner person—open, noncritical listening that is heart to heart, not heart to mind.

I'm encouraged by the number of parents today who have caught on to this and are responding to their children's feelings with knowledgeable compassion. Most of us from earlier generations, however, were raised by people with no notion of this. Children were to be controlled, feelings be damned.

The advanced type of communication that makes a marriage grow in intimacy is not something many of us learned as children. It presumes contact with and acceptance of feelings and a special quality of listening. For both skills, we need boundaries.

Know What Is You and What Is Me

We can't say what we don't know. To tell a spouse about our inner process, we must have contact with it. We need the emotional boundary that comes from knowing intimately who we are, what we want, and how to say it.

To listen uncritically requires knowing that I'm not the other person, that no matter what he says I can keep myself safe, that I can and will limit comments that violate me, and that his process is not my process. It requires the boundary of knowing what is him and what is me.

Marge Gives Up Herself for Bill

Marge and Bill are in their late twenties. They met at a party, spent that night and every available spare minute together for three weeks, and decided to live together. Marge moved into Bill's apartment, which his mother had furnished and decorated. "When you walk in," said Marge, "the color you notice is brown and the impression you get is that of a movie set for an upscale cowboy. The apartment is immaculate and it has no extra space."

Marge gave up her light and airy apartment and stored her few antiques, her family pictures, and most of her books and records in the storage unit in the basement. It occurred to neither one of them to make room for her things or to redo the apartment to make it theirs rather than just his.

Out of joy at being with him, Marge rushed home from work every day to fix a glorious meal. Then Bill took over. He insisted that they eat dinner together at the table, not watching TV or reading, and that he do the dishes. He shopped with her on weekends and instituted what would become their invariable Saturday routine: make love, clean the apartment, do the food shopping, put it away, eat lunch, wash the car, and then bike or walk or run. They then either went for a drive, shopped for the apartment, did something recreational like mini-golf, watched TV, or went to some local event like a boat or gun show.

Marge slipped easily into this routine. Being with Bill gave her a sense of order. Everything was in its place.

Within the first month, however, an odd thing happened. When she lived alone, Marge always used cloth napkins and napkin rings. She would let guests choose a napkin ring and then whenever they came to her place for dinner, she'd put their napkin in the ring they had chosen. One Saturday she went to the storage unit and dug out some napkins and rings, including the one she'd used for several years. She put a napkin in her ring, a crystal circlet, and put it by her place at the table. At dinner, she offered Bill a choice of napkin rings. He pointed to the crystal circlet and said, "I want that one."

Marge felt shocked. She said nothing. It was a small thing really, she told herself. Why should she mind Bill using the napkin ring she'd used for years. After all, she'd had plenty of time to use it and it would still be on the table right in front of her. She'd still see it every day. Nevertheless, as she handed it to him, hiding her reluctance, she felt sad, almost crushed. It seemed so ridiculous to her that she swallowed her tears, sat down, and forced herself to eat dinner.

Another mystery for Marge was the strange sense of unreality she had during her first months in the apartment. Moving through the rooms or cleaning, she felt like she was in a dream. The apartment was luxurious, much more expensive than the one she'd lived in. Maybe, she thought, she just wasn't used to nice things.

It was weird, she thought, the things that felt uncomfortable. Between the heavy furniture, brown tones, and curtained windows (Bill was nearly a fanatic about privacy), the apartment was dark. Although she'd always liked a lot of light, she found it strange that the darkness would bother her so much.

Bill liked his climate controlled. No matter what, he kept the apartment at 68 degrees in the winter, except for the first hour of the morning when he took his shower, and at 72 degrees in the summer. Marge loved open windows, breezes, night sounds.

During their first winter together, Bill came home from work to find that Marge had moved the thermostat to 70 degrees. Without fail, Bill checked the thermostat on awakening, after work, and before bed every day, winter or summer. "Marge, you touched the thermostat," he said.

Immediately Marge felt like a bad girl. She even wanted to deny it. "I was cold," she said.

"You were cold! That doesn't make sense. It was 68 degrees in here. That's plenty warm."

"My period's about to start," she said. "I'm always cold then."

"That's ridiculous," he said.

She could think of nothing to say. Her mind went blank.

"If you're cold you can put on a sweater," he continued. "And that's all there is to it."

Next summer, when Marge wanted to open a window, it led to a three-hour fight. She got her open window that day, but Bill complained about it so much she didn't ask to open a window the rest of the summer.

No Sign of Marge

When Marge moved in, a subtle brainwashing occurred that separated her from her sense of herself, that critical inner awareness we need to be a separate person with a clear emotional boundary. By letting all her things be stored, she moved into an environment that had no sign of her. She lived amid Bill's colors, Bill's furniture, Bill's family pictures.

These are only things, you might say. (Only things! I could answer. We live in the most materialistic society in the world. If our culture prizes anything, it's things.) Things are important, especially things we keep because of their meaning—a trinket from a friend, a memento of a special event, a picture of a loved one. These things are physical extensions of ourselves, they symbolize aspects of our inner selves. Home feels familiar because it contains our things. A motel room feels impersonal because it contains nothing of ourselves (until we strew our clothes and shoes around and make it ours).

Marge was experiencing culture shock. She was surrounded by Bill's things, lighting that was alien to her, Bill's colors and preferences. She slid into Bill's schedule, his standards, his routine, his recreational choices. He even wanted her napkin ring, the only thing in the apartment she had chosen. But Marge couldn't hang on to it. Although she didn't understand how symbolic it was when she handed it to him, her inner self tried to tell her with tears. But she shut them out, cutting herself off from the critical information deep within. Her body knew and wanted to cry out, "I've given up everything that was my own!"

Our Selves Held Hostage

This erosion continued as she submitted herself to Bill's environmental needs. When he belittled her for being cold and she succumbed, she relinquished yet another piece of her physical and emotional identity. Ignoring or denying physical needs erodes our emotional health. Ignoring that we're cold or denying ourselves water when we're thirsty or rest when we're tired sends an express letter to our selves that we aren't important enough to get our basic survival needs met. On the other hand, taking good care of ourselves is incredibly strengthening and promotes intactness.

As Marge succumbed to Bill's compulsive need for control, even over whether a window was open or shut, she slowly put herself into a hostage situation. She gave Bill control over her basic physical needs.

A hostage has a single goal, to survive until escape or rescue. Toward that end a subtle psychological shift occurs. The hostage bonds with the person in control. She starts seeing things from the controller's perspective. She comes to understand how the controller thinks and, out of loyalty, may even side with him against others. Her identity may become so submerged beneath that of the controller that she comes to fear being without him; she will sabotage rescue efforts and refuse to escape.

Survival Eclipses Development

Children held hostage by abusive parents and wives of abusive husbands clearly demonstrate this process. Focusing on survival always eclipses development. How can your self-awareness expand if you're cold or if light deprivation is robbing you of energy? If you are worried about being hit, what do you do with your outrage? Are you safe enough to express it? What are you learning about anger?

Intimacy comes from being known, and being known requires

knowing yourself, having a self to know, and having enough of a sense of your own individuality to have something to present to the other.

Even if you have a self, intimacy takes time, openness, nonjudgment, talking, listening, and acceptance. There's a vast difference between intimacy and infatuation. Said W. Somerset Maugham: "Love is what happens to men and women who don't know each other."

Intimacy Requires Two People

The most critical ingredient for intimacy between two people is that there be two people. True intimacy requires two separate individuals. Symbiosis is not intimacy. When two people team up because they aren't whole separately, they have not created intimacy. They haven't even created a whole person.

Making the transition from two needy people to two distinct people intimately bonded takes lots of time, arguments, communication, mistakes, clarity, forgiveness, acceptance, and support. If the two have worked hard on their individual development before their commitment to each other, this process takes less time than if they're starting from scratch as they walk out of the church.

Let's face it, lots of people get married to fix something that hurts. There's quite a distance between this motivation and the development of true intimacy.

People may marry for myriad reasons—to escape home, to not be lonely, to get taken care of, to get kids taken care of, to have a companion, to improve financial resources, to have someone to share things with, as a statement to others that one is chosen, to feel wanted, to meet social expectations. Within seconds of being married, a change happens.

Before the rice has gummed up the sidewalk, each person's childhood issues start flowing out, issues about power, individuality, control, separateness, and intimacy. Since many couples are anticipating a peaceful slide into happily-ever-after, this turmoil comes as a shock. He's supposed to love me more than anyone else in the world and he wants to read the paper while he eats breakfast. She used to be so undemanding and now she wants to talk for hours about "our issues" when I come home tired from work. Seemingly small things trigger huge reactions, and each person wonders who this stranger is that seemed so appealing a few short weeks ago.

It's as though the marriage certificate has an agenda printed on the back and this agenda presents to the couple a list lifted right out of their childhood families, a list that says, do this, don't do this, this will be critical, this won't matter. Each partner has a list and important items will conflict with each other.

Laura's Story

The first time I saw Tim, he was standing in a pulpit about to preach a sermon. I was impressed with him before he even put the "Amen" on the end of his opening prayer. There was something about him, an honesty, a freshness, I can't explain it, but I felt drawn to him.

We were both there accidentally. My friend had invited me to her Thanksgiving Eve service. Tim, I found out afterwards, was from another church. Usually I scoot away after services, but this time I let her lead us to the parish hall and a potluck dinner.

I was arranging celery when he walked through the door. I didn't notice him, but he noticed me. A hand reached for a piece of celery, I looked up, and there he was. "Need any help?" he said.

"I have to get the radishes on here somehow."

He smiled, "I'll be right back." He disappeared and then returned to my side of the table. "I had to wash my hands," he explained, "been shaking all those hands."

He pulled up a chair beside me and together we balanced radishes that insisted on rolling down the celery sticks and launching onto the table. People who have been infatuated can understand the intoxicating fun this was. Ordinarily, arranging radishes is not that thrilling.

He called and we had a date. He didn't even touch me. After all the paws I've picked off my body, this was a wonderful change. In fact, I experienced something new. I wanted him. I wanted his kiss. I wanted his touch.

We began to see each other regularly. He was so happy to be with me. He liked me. He wanted to be in my presence. He was proud of me. He wanted me to meet his friends.

I liked his boyishness and enthusiasm. Most of all, I felt completely safe with him because he wanted me so much. That feeling of safety ruled out all other thoughts. He was so wildly happy just being with me that I felt very secure. For that security, I would have followed him anywhere.

I didn't know that I was carrying with me from my first weeks of life a tremendous fear of abandonment. I didn't know that the key to my heart was to assuage that fear.

We married. I felt very nervous about the ceremony. I kept talking myself into it. Later, my therapist said it would have been okay to delay the ceremony until I was ready.

But I'm used to making myself go through with things. I've never been ready for the things that have happened to me. I wasn't ready to be born, but I came early. I wasn't ready to be alone at birth, but I was alone until they took me out of the incubator. I wasn't ready to leave my grandmother when my mother took me from her home. I wasn't ready for sex when my stepfather started touching me. I wasn't ready to be married to Tim, but he wanted me so much that I wanted that to be enough. I could never have hurt his feelings by saying I needed more time.

The first months of marriage were wonderful for me because my fear was gone. I had this constant sense of unreality, but I didn't think to question it. It never occurred to me that I felt this way because it wasn't my life I was living. I wouldn't realize that until later.

I lived in a fairy tale called "The Preacher's Wife" and got a lot of attention for being the star at all the social events. Members of his congregation would hug and compliment us. I smiled and smiled.

Blessed by God, our union would be perfect not only for us but be the Marriage Symbolic to the people. My feet didn't touch the ground for a month. I thought I should feel thrilled with all this, but I didn't. It didn't feel real. I have good instincts but I don't listen to them. I told myself this was fun and I should go along with it. But my instincts said there would be a price.

When we married I didn't know much about Tim's financial situation. I assumed he was taken care of by the church and that he handled money well. I also made the mistake of idealizing him.

Right before we married, he took me shopping. We went to a furniture store and had great fun roaming the aisles, plopping on chairs, and finding out what we both liked. He surprised me when he said, "What do you want in our house?"

"You have furniture already. So do I."

"But this will be our house," he said. "Pick out what you like."

It was another heady experience. His generosity bolstered my feeling of safety. He would take care of me. Growing up, I got a minimum of care and even less than that when my stepfather entered the picture. More than anything else in the world, I wanted to be taken care of.

Tim would hold me for hours. I couldn't get enough of it. After no affection growing up, I soaked up his affection like a dusty plant. He gave me three things I'd been starved for my whole life—the security of being wanted, the safety of being taken care of, and all the affection I asked for.

Did I love him? Did I want to give to him? I skipped over these questions. I would have done anything to secure what he gave me.

He took me out a lot. I liked not cooking. We went to movies and on little trips.

The first crack in paradise came when he came home one day with a bunch of things we didn't need. He had driven by a garage sale on the way home. He'd picked stuff that was broken or ill-suited for our house. He was pleased because he'd gotten it all for $5.

We didn't fight. I told myself it wasn't a big deal. But it bothered me because it was such a waste. We wouldn't be able to use the things. I started to feel a little afraid, but I suppressed it.

A month later, he came home with a new TV set, a month after that, a VCR, in another month, a different car. This car wasn't better than the one he'd had before. It was actually older and more worn, but he'd driven by it on the way home and had fallen in love with it.

Warning bells had begun to sound. Did we have the money for all these purchases? He was secretive about money and he didn't like me to question him. I walked into his study while he was paying the bills and he yelled at me to get out. Fear tore through me again. I talked myself out of it.

I wasn't paying attention one day and opened a bill that was his. It was a charge card bill and it had big warnings because he had missed payments the last two months. He was furious that I'd seen it, but I insisted that he explain what was going on.

He minimized it. He'd gotten a little behind because he'd had to borrow money to pay his taxes. As a minister, he had to pay self-employment tax and he'd had trouble making the payment the last few years, just a discipline he hadn't caught on to yet. So while he

had those loans, he was a little short on spending money. He'd
wanted to wine and dine me and he was so happy he couldn't let
this pinch interfere with his desire to show me a special time. He'd
charged a few things and missed a few payments.

Not to worry. He'd catch up.

The fear that he'd chased away came back. I didn't know this in
any very conscious way, but the safety I'd married him to get began
drifting away. I'd married him to feel safe. The whole situation that
was growing around money showed me that he wasn't as together as
I'd thought. Unknowingly, I had made a contract with him. He
would keep me feeling safe and I would make him happy. He was
breaking my invisible contract.

He stopped holding me so much. I had an almost insatiable need
for contact. I didn't understand that his withdrawal was connected
to feeling so much financial pressure. All I knew was that I had a
desperate need to be held and he was always too busy to do it. He
had meetings to prepare for and sermons to write. He needed a lot
of time alone in his study. I began to feel less important than the
church. Anyone in the congregation could call him at any time and
get his undivided attention. This had shades of my grandmother's
involvement in charity work that left me lonely at home. I'd peek in
the study and he'd be reading the Bible. What kind of demanding
witch interrupts a man reading a Bible? His activities, like my
grandmother's, seemed so worthy. Who was I to want attention from
someone involved in such holy pursuits?

He acted like it was a strain if I asked him to hold me for five
minutes. Our sex life waned.

He broke the second provision of my unstated contract. He was to
hold me as much as I needed and he wasn't doing it.

I wasn't happy in the marriage. I had married him to get rid of
the fear. I had married him because he had been so enthusiastic
about me, I was certain he would never abandon me. My unwritten
contract with him was that he would not abandon me in any way.
But his preoccupation with the church and with money left me
abandoned. I was afraid again.

I got obsessed with money. I thought if I could get him to handle
money differently, he would come back to me. I tried to reform his
spending. My enemy was impulsive buying. To buy something was
to create an additional financial obligation, which created pressure.
Eliminate the buying, eliminate the pressure. I used every method

known to woman to influence his spending—tears, threats, anger, sex, coddling, food, seduction, persuasion, logic. Nothing worked. As I saw how little control over this I had, I got angrier, more frightened, and more obsessed. I used my money to pay for all our needs thinking this would free his money to pay off his bills. This freed his money to buy more things.

He maxed his credit cards and I started using mine to finance the lifestyle we'd started. I insisted we go to therapy and my entire focus was his spending. I learned about compulsive spending and I insisted he go to Twelve Step meetings and get recovery. He went once and didn't like it.

In all this time, I was unaware of my own obsession with him. I became a bitch. I was so angry that I was constantly after him. Nothing he did was good enough. Sometimes I wanted to punish him. I don't think I really knew why. I thought I had a reason—I wanted to punish him for putting us in such a precarious financial condition. But now I think his abandoning me opened a door to all the anger I didn't dare feel toward my mother and grandmother.

He was a stand-in for them. He did what they did and he was going to get the venom I'd stored for them all these years.

Eventually I drove him away. I don't blame myself for all of it—he had something to do with it. But taking his inventory didn't get me anywhere. When he first left, I needed a lot of people to tell me that his final abandonment was because of who he was, not because I was unworthy.

But the truth was, I had a lot of responsibility for the way things turned out and until I looked at that and worked on myself, nothing changed for me.

An Adult, But Not a Whole Person

Laura's boundary development was hampered from birth. A victim of the hands-off policy that was then standard treatment for premature babies, she never bonded with her mother and so lagged in developing a sense of her physical self. This touch deprivation continued through her childhood.

Laura's mother's absence and her grandmother's busyness also left her emotionally abandoned. She had at best a superficial connection to her family, but lost even this when her mother uprooted her from her grandmother's home and took her to the house where her stepfather sexually abused her. This prolonged lack of mental and emotional contact prevented important self-development. The natural dependency needs all children have were not met, and her preoccupation with survival caused her to bypass the normal flow of developmental tasks. By the time she was an adult, she was not a whole person.

Lured by Safety

Laura grew with a distorted sense of physical boundaries and incomplete emotional boundaries. Such a condition creates fear. Many survivors of incest, abuse, neglect, or abandonment live with fear. This fear may not be conscious, but the prospect of being hurt again governs many choices. Survivors commonly pick mates who seemingly chase the fear away only to discover themselves reliving the same pattern of abuse or abandonment.

Two people with incomplete self-development and unhealthy boundaries find each other, find relief in each other, and then find hell with each other. Many times these relationships break up and each person moves on to another person only to repeat the cycle.

Subsequent partners may appear to be very different from each other but some similar underlying subconscious effect is very likely perpetuated. If a person's greatest need is the removal of fear, what these partners will have in common is the initial ability to make the fear leave. Perhaps one is centered and joyful, another is powerful, another has a big house. These are very different attributes but each in its own way can give a person a feeling of safety. What one marries is the feeling of safety but when that feeling is lost, the basis for the relationship is lost.

The relationship doesn't then end abruptly, however. The failure of safety enables both parties to express the feelings repressed when safety was finally lost. That this is the underlying cause of many an argument goes unnoticed. Most of us are unaware of how powerfully we are influenced by the need to express feelings we have actively suppressed.

My guess is that many of the ills of the world—violence, crime, rape, war, abuse, bigotry, oppression—result from the inability of individuals to handle their own feelings in a healthy way. But I digress, intimacy is the issue here.

Two Paths: Survival or Development

Let me simply present the building blocks of a whole human

being. A growing child is presented with one of two paths, survival or development. If a child is abused, neglected, abandoned, ignored, or made to assume adult responsibilities, she must focus her attention and energy on survival. Whatever relief she gets from insuring survival, she gets to use on development. If all her energy goes toward surviving, development will get short shrift.

A child whose basic physical needs are met ascends to another level of needs. A baby who gets enough sleep, food, and diaper changing also needs to be held and spoken to. He needs the stimulation of colors and sounds. A toddler who gets enough food and rest also needs to move around, to explore in safety, and to be held. A young child who gets nutritious meals and sufficient rest and exercise also needs to ask a lot of questions, to take things apart, and to explore his own body. A ten-year-old child who is safe and sufficiently fed and clothed also needs mental stimulation, an appropriate level of responsibility, social activities, skill training, interpretation of complicated events, help being safely alone, conversation, communication, and listening. In each case, healthy independence appropriate to the age level emerges when dependency needs are fulfilled.

If a child is not chronically frightened and confused, he is free to expand into the developmental tasks presented to him as he grows up. If most of her attention is focused on surviving, important phases of development will be missed.

Stored Feelings Control Us

This has two enormous consequences. The full emergence of self is harmed. And powerful feelings about the harm and the need for survival get stored.

Stored feelings control us. They unconsciously influence our values, decisions, perspectives, and especially our choice of mates. They determine the types of defenses we'll construct to make up for poor boundaries.

We reverse the damage done to us as children by reversing this process—unlocking feelings, meeting basic physical needs, getting dependency and other developmental needs met, and building boundaries. The harmed self can then become whole.

If We Don't Have Boundaries We Need Defenses

A whole person presents a completely different possibility in relationships than an incomplete person. A whole person can define needs, express feelings, and set limits. A whole person maintains a separate identity with boundaries rather than defenses.

A boundary comes from an awareness of one's distinctness from another. The ability to build one arises from finishing unfinished childhood agendas. Identifying the harm, feeling the suppressed feelings, and grieving the losses restore wholeness to the incomplete child living inside us. As this work is done, one's capacity for intimacy expands.

Laura's Story

The thing that really made the most dramatic difference (and I built up to this with four years of therapy) was going back to the first weeks of my life and grieving the horrible abandonment I experienced then. It's the hardest thing I've ever done. Unlike a lot of people, I'm not afraid to feel and I'm not afraid of therapy. I usually jump right into it. I'll tell you, though, the weeks of mourning my early days of babyhood were so hard, I could see why I used people, food, and compulsive working to avoid it all those years. Some days I was so limp with grief I could only lie in bed and breathe. Then I went through another phase of being so angry I'd beat on my bed and scream.

It changed my life. I stopped needing another person to take care of me. I didn't need someone else to fill me so I'd feel like a whole person.

I began loving someone and I really loved. I didn't have a contract hidden away inside me. I didn't have to inventory faults because that wasn't my business (and my survival was no longer linked to another's perfection). I felt a flow of closeness and distance between us and could handle that within myself instead of demanding constant togetherness.

This is all so different. It's not what I thought intimacy would be. I thought it would be like a fairy tale, but this feels real, not like a fantasy. I'm not floating, I'm grounded. We're bonded, but not in bondage to each other's needs or ideas. We're alike in many ways and different too. I'm comfortable with our differences. Our arguments can get pretty hot but they aren't scary. In a pretty short time we can work our way to realizing that we're seeing something differently but that each view is valid. I remember how I struggled to get Tim to see things my way and he never could. But I never saw how he looked at things either.

Here's something amazing. I've never felt more secure in my life. Here I was trying to get Tim to keep giving me that feeling of safety, and now I have that feeling all the time. No one gives it to me though. I get it through myself.

Bonded But Not in Bondage

When we feel our emotional boundaries, we can discriminate between our feelings and another's feelings. We can hear another's feelings and not have to fix them. We can discern what issues are ours and what issues belong to the other person. We can protect ourselves from being dumped on when someone else can't handle his feelings. We can refuse to take responsibility when it rightly belongs to the other guy.

Owning Our Stuff

People commonly handle uncomfortable feelings by shoving them onto someone else or by getting someone else to take responsibility for them.

I come through the door anxious about a client and soon discover that the house is out of toilet paper. I rant, "Why can't someone else in this household keep up with supplies!"

What am I really doing? I'm handling my anxiety by turning it into anger against innocent bystanders. I'm getting them to take care of something that is actually my responsibility.

One alternative is to be conscious of my feelings and actions and take responsibility as soon as possible. For example, "Oops, I'm yelling at you and you didn't do anything wrong. Forgive me. I'm really upset about something else. Excuse me while I call the person I talk to about these things."

Another grand alternative is to pick a mate who also has boundaries, someone who refuses to let you dump feelings inappropriately.

"Damn it, why can't you buy toilet paper?"

"Hold it! I didn't do anything wrong. If you want me to do something, just ask. Your anger doesn't fit this problem. If you want to talk about what's really going on, I'll listen."

Such a response can be maddening, but a partner who refuses to enable unhealthy behavior—and fighting about a bogus issue is unhealthy because solving it doesn't solve the main problem—is a partner who participates in restoring clarity to the relationship. Dealing with real issues saves lots of time. Also, wasting time on distractions keeps confusion in the relationship and increases the possibility that partners will hurt each other out of escalating anger and frustration.

There's an incredible difference between anger surrounding a real issue and anger generated around scapegoating issues. When the issue is genuine and from the heart, the anger doesn't burn, it isn't scary. When anger is being diverted from some other person or issue, it scalds. It creates new problems in the relationship that would not have to be there if the true feelings and problems had been communicated. Such a mess can make us feel involved, but this involvement is not intimacy. Many of us grew up in families where arguments provided the only sense of attachment. If we're screaming at each other, we're involved for the moment, sure. But this compares poorly with the peaceful connectedness of true intimacy.

So how does a boundary work in an intimate relationship?

Laura's Story

I woke up this morning and before I was even conscious I could tell Lee wanted to make love. I started feeling pressured and my eyes weren't even open yet. I guess I learned to have this radar even in my sleep, from needing to know if my stepfather was in the room.

I started to feel angry about it. Lee knew I had an important meeting scheduled and I needed to keep focused on that until it was over. I could feel myself start to withdraw, my favorite tool to handle anger.

Then I suddenly remembered I had boundaries. I pictured that I was me and separate from Lee. I thought about what I wanted and needed. I wanted to keep my mental energies focused on the meeting and until then I needed to be separate. I needed to stay within my own consciousness.

I had this filling out feeling. A good feeling. A feeling of being there, of being myself. The old me would have been so filled with Lee's needs of me, that my sense of myself would have been overshadowed. This new me felt more and more distinct. I felt who I was. I knew I could meet my need to stay focused on my task. I could protect myself. My anger went away. I had no need to withdraw.

Lee can want me, but I don't have to do anything about it. That

want is a feeling within a separate human being. It's not my feelin͘
this instant. I don't have to have the same feeling. I don't have to fix
that feeling. Lee gets to handle wanting me. It's not my job. I don't
have to be mad that that feeling exists or make it go away.

I looked at Lee and saw that we were separate, that this person
was a completely distinct human being with feelings and outlooks
that were unique and could function without my interference. I
haven't the right to exert control over this other human being. I am
privileged to receive this person's regard.

Each time I have this awareness I also feel a deepening of my
love. I used to think intimacy meant being blended with the other.
Now I feel the opposite. We are very separate so our coming
together is a tremendous blessing and a gift.

I'm surprised the difference this makes to our lovemaking.
Touching feels so very good. It doesn't do what Tim's holding did.
When Tim held me, I could feel these empty spaces in my soul
getting relief. I felt starved for it. When Lee holds me, it's nourish-
ing but not life and death. It's much better though. Because we are
clearly separate, our togetherness is incredibly enriching. Maybe I
can't explain this.

When We Don't Have Boundaries

Laura illustrates how one shifts from an accustomed
boundaryless/defensive response to an awareness of one's boundaries. If we don't have boundaries, we need defenses such as withdrawal, control, sidetracking, creating rules, trying to make
something the other's fault, humor, sex, rationalizing, intellectualiz-
ing, name calling, perfectionism, black-white thinking, threats,
bringing up some other issue, coldness, sweetness, excessive
concern for the other—all are handy ways to avoid feeling and to
avoid communication. The healthy alternative is to state true
feelings.

Here's an incident in which defenses were used.

Jerry versus Ellen

"I love you deeply," said Jerry.

"I've got to pick up the kids," said Ellen.

Jerry stomped out of the room and out to the garage and started
changing the oil in his car. When Ellen said good-bye, he grunted
an answer.

Ellen felt the coldness in his grunt and drove away mad at him and the world. She always had to do everything herself. She'd get the kids, clean the house, cook the supper. He was always working on that damn car. He'd probably want to have sex tonight. No way could she feel interested in that. She didn't feel the least bit close to him. He didn't know squat about what she was going through.

Let's replay this with boundaries.

Jerry and Ellen
"I love you," said Jerry.

"I've got to pick up the kids," said Ellen.

"Wait a minute," said Jerry. "Did you hear what I said?"

"Did you say something?"

"Yes, I said I loved you. I want you to hear that. I want you to pause for just a minute and take that in. Then go for the kids."

She looked at him. "I want to, but I feel so pressured. I've got a million things to do before Mom gets here."

"Hey, you're not alone. I can help."

"I've got to get the kids and go to the store and get the food fixed and in the oven and clean the house and transplant the tomatoes."

"It doesn't have to be perfect," he said. "We could get cold meat and salad from the deli, get the kids to help us pick up the living room, do the tomatoes tomorrow, and sit on the porch drinking Perrier with lime and wiggling our toes before she arrives. I could go to the deli while you get the kids."

She smiled. "I want to pick out the food."

He laughed. "I'll get the kids and sic them on the living room."

"I love you," she said, really seeing him.

"I love you," he said, receiving it. "Don't forget the Perrier and limes."

It Doesn't Have to Be Perfect
Is this really possible in an imperfect world? Boundaries make the difference. In the second interchange, Jerry and his love were intact regardless of Ellen's response. Her busyness was a separate event from his feeling of love. Jerry was clear about what he wanted, another part of having a boundary. He could communicate that he wanted her to take in his message, but he didn't need to control her

or make her do it. And he remained intact after saying what he wanted even though she couldn't give it to him.

Ellen was able to get in touch with herself and see that although she wanted to receive Jerry's love, she felt too pressured to be open to him. She could tell him these things, thereby acknowledging both herself and him, and getting the problem out into the open.

Jerry's self-esteem continued to be intact. He was able to switch to her feeling of stress, look at her problem, let her needs have priority over his original desire to be taken in, and offer alternatives to getting things done.

Ellen then was able to let go of the idea that things had to be done a certain way. She could share the work with him. Her selfness was not tied up in doing all the work herself, cooking an elaborate meal, and having her house perfect for her mother. The pressure thus taken off, she could be open to him, take him in, and feel her love for him. Invigorated by what was no more than a minute of intimacy, both went off into the rest of the day.

So, intimacy is simple. For two whole people with good boundaries who have taken care of their childhood agendas and can communicate true feelings and issues while remaining intact, it's a snap. Intimacy will grow with time and commitment.

You want this? Read on.

CHAPTER NINE

MENDING WALL

How to Build Boundaries

It's never too late to build boundaries for yourself. No matter what kind of mess your life is in, healthy boundaries will improve it. Do the following three things and your boundaries can't help but improve:

- Increase your self-awareness.
- Identify childhood violations and the offenders, feel about them, and get care for that damage.
- Examine the state of your boundaries in your present relationships and clean them up.

Sound simple? It's simple but not easy. The rest of this chapter consists of exercises that can help you with these three challenges. You can work on these in any order or on all three at once. As you delve into one aspect of boundary building, the other two will be helped. For example, as you become more aware of yourself, you very likely will realize more and more ways your boundaries were violated as a child. As you heal from these violations, internal boundaries will grow and you'll find yourself creating boundaries in present relationships.

Tell some trusted friends what you are doing and ask for their support. They can help by listening as you make new discoveries, caring when it's hard, and cheering you on when you take a new risk.

Increase Your Awareness of Yourself

Build your self-concept. Build your awareness of what's you and what's not you.

Exercise 9.1

1. Get a small notebook and keep it with you.
2. For one week, research the ways you're different from the people around you.
3. Notice every time your opinion differs from the person you are with. Jot a brief note in your notebook describing your actual opinion. Notice every time your values differ from the person you are with. Make a note of it. Notice when your preference is different. List your preference.

4. At the end of the week, read your notebook.
5. Discuss this process with a trusted friend, one who listens well. Don't discuss this with a friend who tries to make her opinions yours.

Exercise 9.2

1. Watch a talk show on television. When you agree with a statement, say so. When you disagree, tell the television your opinion. Gesture, raise your voice, let Oprah get an earful of your views on the matter.
2. Discuss this process with a good friend.

Exercise 9.3

1. At a party or event at which you are interacting with an acquaintance, notice when you disagree with her.
2. Tell her you disagree and then state your own view.
3. When the interaction is finished, excuse yourself and go to a room where you can sit down and recover from the stress of the interaction.
4. As soon as possible, talk to a trusted friend about your experience.

Exercise 9.4

1. Disagree with a friend. Notice when your view differs and say so.
2. It's okay to say how hard it is or to express your feeling about disagreeing with her:
   "This is hard for me to say. I see it differently than you do."
   "It's scary for me to say this. I disagree with you about that."
   "I value your opinion. Mine's different in this case."
3. When the interaction is completed, discuss with her or another friend how you felt.

Exercise 9.5

1. For 24 hours, pay attention to how you react to your needs. If you are thirsty, do you get yourself something to drink immedi-

ately, do you delay and take care of something else first, or do you ignore that need? If you are tired, do you rest or push harder? If you need for someone to listen to you, do you ask for it or do you squelch your need? If you need affection, do you ask for it? If you ignore your needs, what do you do to make up for this subtle abuse? Do you eat, drink, or shop to console yourself for being neglected?

Pay attention to both your physical and emotional needs. Every time you meet any need, give yourself a star. Any time you deny or ignore a need, give yourself a minus.

At the end of the 24-hour period, add up the stars and minuses. How's your need-meeting quotient?

2. For the next 24 hours, deliberately meet every physical need as soon as possible. If you're tired at work, for example, figure out a way to give yourself a little bit of a break. Walk in the garden, close the door and rest your head on your desk, go to the employee's lounge and stretch out for five minutes.

   At the end of the 24 hours, how do you feel about yourself? What difference did it make for you to respond to your needs?

3. Talk this over with a trusted friend.

4. For the next 24 hours, meet each emotional need as quickly and as richly as possible. If you need someone to listen, call a friend and ask for that. If you need affection, ask a good person for a hug. If you need to be alone, arrange that. If you need to be in the healing presence of someone who cares a lot about you, arrange that.

   At the end of the 24 hours, notice how you feel about yourself. What difference did it make for you to respond to your emotional needs?

5. Talk all this over with a trusted friend or therapist.

6. Talk to your friend and your therapist about what it would take to be able to continue meeting physical and emotional needs day after day. Repeat steps 2 through 5, extending the time period to a week.

7. Talk to your friend and your therapist about the thoughts that emerge that block you from caring for yourself this way. If you are in therapy, spend some time attending to these blocks. Removing them will free you to be good to yourself.

   As you get better at responding to your needs, you may notice two things. One, that responding to needs is in the long run very efficient. A bit of rest when you first feel tired means you won't need lots of rest later when you are completely spent. Two, that meeting needs gives a feeling of strength and wholeness, which develops boundaries.

Identify Childhood Violations

Working out childhood boundary violations is delicate toil. A therapist wise in the ways of boundaries can provide immeasurable help. She or he can guide you in discovering just what violations were committed and how that harm influences today. A good therapist can provide safety so that you can experience your full range of feelings about the ways you were violated.

When you skinned your knee as a child, it felt so much better when someone helped you up and washed off the dirt and said soothing words. Boundary violations feel better when someone helps you up and washes off the dirt and shows care.

Healing the damage can take a long time. If you spent seventeen years in a dysfunctional family, you could have been exposed to 20 boundary violations every day. That amounts to 123,100 boundary violations.

Even though we've spent 24 hours a day for 30 or 40 years feeling unsafe in a dysfunctional family, it takes only an hour or two of therapy a week for maybe six or seven years to heal the damage. Perhaps that sounds like a lot of therapy to you, but what you get in exchange is immeasurable—a new life, gratifying relationships, and confidence in your own being.

Exercise 9.6

1. List the people who were important to you or who seemed powerful to you when you were a child. For example, Mom, Dad, Uncle Fred, big brother Tom, Aunt Winnie.
2. List the violations or fuzzy boundaries you received from each person. Include violations of distance and intrusion and emotional as well as physical violations.
   Remember, neglect of your emotional self is a violation. Include triangulation, being expected to help with adult problems, and any way you had to take care of Mom or any adult beyond what's appropriate for a child.

3. Take this list to your therapy session, or reserve a few private hours with a trusted friend. Let yourself feel your anger and sadness about these violations. Talk about the losses you've suffered as a result. Allow yourself to be comforted for these losses.
4. After this session, take the rest of the day off. Do something pleasant and undemanding—a walk, a stroll in a garden, curling up with herb tea and your favorite music. Rest. You've done very well.
5. Sometimes it's necessary to do this kind of inventory several times. Sometimes therapy becomes an ongoing inventory of ancient and potent violations. As we get stronger, we become aware of more from our pasts. Each time you garner the courage to explore, speak, feel, and be comforted, your inner self will be strengthened and internal boundaries will grow.

Clean Up Your Present Boundaries

Examine relationships with dependents. Look at your interactions with your children, your subordinates at work, your clients, or any other people in your care. Are you acting as a peer in any of these relationships?

Are you looking for friendship from your children? Are you looking for the nurturing of a parent from your child? Your child cannot be your peer or your parent. The time does come when care-taking switches, when your children will make difficult decisions regarding your care, but until you are physically or mentally unable to care for yourself, your children should be focused on meeting their needs, not yours. Of course you need friendship. Friends are the people who can meet this need.

Are you participating as a peer in activities with clients or subordinates? Do you talk about your personal problems with your support staff or with clients? Do you have dinner with your staff frequently? Do you share many social functions with clients? Do you invite confidences from your support staff?

Such actions muddy boundaries. Discuss your personal concerns with friends, peers, clergy, in recovery groups, or with a therapist. Let your subordinates get help from the same sources. If one day you're a shoulder for your supervisee and the next day you must correct him, it's hard for both of you. The special trust and openness that grows between people who share confidences is shattered by interaction that reminds everyone the company is first.

If you turn to a client for help with personal issues, she will probably turn to you less and less. After all, she's coming to you for help or for a service. You will be sabotaging the purpose of the relationship and very likely lose the person as a client.

Many people carry on social lives with clients. It's a common American thing to do. How then is this a boundary issue?

Linda Thorn, a minister, and her husband socialize with Joan and Art Miller, a couple from the church. They have dinner frequently and play cards together. The women become good friends. They take a brief trip together, share confidences, and have lots of fun. Then Art visits Linda in her office at the church. He confides that he's been seeing another woman. He plans to keep on seeing her. He's not sure whether he will tell his wife or not. Art is approaching Linda in her capacity as pastoral counselor and spiritual advisor. Linda's loyalty to her friend Joan muddies the situation.

You are an attorney. Esther Long consults you regarding her will. She names you as trustee. She can't afford to pay you so she offers to trade her services as a gardener. You agree that she will landscape your yard and maintain it in return for drawing up the will and administering the estate in the event of her death. She doesn't have much actual cash, but she has principle tied up in trusts that will be distributed in portions to her children for ten years after her death. You make the will.

Throughout the summer, Esther proves to be unreliable. She doesn't show up when she says she will. The grass grows too long and makes your office look shoddy. She doesn't weed the flowers very thoroughly, so long grasses stick out among the petunias, and dead flowers hang on the bushes. Your irritation with her grows. She rips out a clematis, thinking it to be a weed, a clematis your grandmother planted fifty years ago. Then she dumps fertilizer in the middle of the yard, which burns a spot six feet in diameter. You finally decide to tell her you are no longer willing to be her trustee, but before you can do so she dies. You're stuck administering the estate for ten years. The burn spot stays in the lawn for five years.

Imagine if you were Esther's therapist in the above situation and you were supposed to be warm and accepting while she was wreaking havoc with your yard. Imagine if you were Esther's friend and you were employing her to do the yard. What would happen to the friendship?

Crossing advocate or supervisory roles with peer activities often leads to this type of boundary confusion. Sooner or later something happens that demands one type of response from an advocate or supervisor and another type from a friend or peer.

So what do you do if you live in a small town or on an island? The number of people available for friendships, clients, and employees is limited. If you have no choice but to blur boundaries to meet your social and relationship needs, know that sooner or later a boundary issue will develop. These guidelines can be defied, but in so doing you open yourself to consequences that can result in a resentful employee or in the loss of the person as both friend and client.

Examine relationships with people who give you care, advocacy, or supervision. Are you seeking friendship with your supervisor, your therapist, your clergyperson, or your attorney? Sooner or later the roles will conflict. Hopefully your therapist keeps good boundaries and you can talk to her about your desire for friendship with her. A boundary-wise therapist will help you explore the issues that prompt this wish while keeping a very clean limit on the therapeutic relationship.

Is your supervisor a good friend? Imagine this. Because she's your friend you told her how important your coming vacation is. Your marriage is shaky and you are counting on this time with your husband to renew the intimacy that's been lost. Two days before your vacation, however, she cancels it. She says she absolutely has to have you at work. Something critical is coming up and you're the only one who can do it. What happens to your friendship? What happens to your loyalty to her as a boss?

Is your attorney a good friend to you and your husband? What if your husband decides he wants a divorce and the kids, and your attorney represents him?

Is your doctor a close friend? What if she thinks you absolutely must have a radical mastectomy and you want a second opinion?

Get the picture? When advocacy and peer roles are mixed, loyalties become divided. Life is bound to present a sticky situation that will weaken both positions. In the end, you may lose both an advocate and a friend.

Examine relationships with peers. Sticky situations can come from:
- Employing a friend
- Selling a service or an item to a friend
- Buying a service or item from a friend
- A close relationship with both partners of a marriage. If you share confidences with both of them, can you trust one to keep what you say from the other? If one shares a confidence that would hurt the other, what do you do?

How to Clean Up Boundaries

So you've examined your relationships and confusion reigns. You have peer and advocacy and care receiver relationships mixed up willy-nilly. You didn't know any better. You're a good person.

1. In each case where roles are mixed, decide which role is more valuable to you.
2. Talk to your friend about your discovery and tell him what change you'd like.
3. If he's heard of boundaries, he'll catch on fairly quickly. If boundaries are foreign to him, he may need to read this book. Give him some time to catch up to you and to tell you what he wants.
4. Negotiate your new relationship. You'll both derive the greatest benefit if you both reveal all your feelings and listen to the other.

For instance, if your attorney, Sally, is your best friend, what do you want most? If you need Sally as an attorney more than as a friend, talk to her about it. Explain you've read a book that has shown you the pitfalls inherent in blending roles. You love Sally, but you need her most as an attorney. You would like to make your relationship more professional.

She may feel hurt or rejected. She may counter with negotiation. She'd rather be your friend than your attorney. She knows a couple of lawyers who are very good. Would you consider switching to them and keeping the friendship?

Decide what you really want. Say that. It takes honesty and courage to work out these relationship issues. If Sally is healthy and honest, you can reach a place where both of you feel good about the evolution of the relationship.

What if your boss or supervisor is the one who keeps promoting social activities? What if your boss invites you to confide in her about personal matters?

Explain that you've realized it isn't good for you to mix your personal life with work. It could interfere with your effectiveness as an employee. To prevent that, you've decided to participate only in activities that directly relate to your job. The company picnic is fine. Lunch with an account is fine. But you've decided to keep personal information to yourself and to relate to your boss on a professional basis. If your boss is healthy and tuned in, she'll get it. If she isn't, that's not your problem.

What if you fear that her lack of health will threaten your job? Check it out with a therapist. She can help you discern the reality of the situation. An unhealthy supervisor can trigger responses first provoked by an unhealthy parent. A therapist can help you get clear on what you must do now to be safe and what past issues are influencing your reactions.

Disease in the organization. It's a fact of life that some bosses are very unhealthy and abuse their power, sometimes unknowingly, to get their needs met. Unhealthiness in the boss shows up throughout the organization. I'm amazed that more companies aren't aware of the pyramidal effect of their failure to select healthy managers. A non-recovering alcoholic, codependent, or compulsive manager can have a detrimental effect on subordinates she never sees. By the same token, a supervisor in therapy can lift up her entire department.

If disease is rampant in your organization, you can try to develop a healthy base with your coworkers and to promote a healthy relationship with your supervisor. As you get healthy, the people around you may begin to relate to you in healthier ways without knowing why. With good boundaries, it's possible to be relatively unaffected by the turmoil around you. You can be an island of calm within the maelstrom.

Sometimes, however, you need to change jobs or departments. But now you know what to look for—a healthy supervisor in an organization where communication is welcome, recovery is honored, and boundaries are respected.

Cleaning up boundaries with parents and children. If you've been taking care of your parents, you can resign (unless they are truly unable to care for themselves; even so, caretaking can be assigned to someone else). Confront them. If they don't get it, take care of yourself.

You know better than I the devices your parents use to keep things as they are. Some parents respond to honest confrontation. Some are willing to accompany their children to therapy to fix the relationship, and some need to experience your unwillingness to continue in the old ways before they understand that you're serious. Sadly, some parents are so afraid or so damaged by addictions or dysfunctional lives that they've lost the capacity for honesty. *People of the Lie*, by M. Scott Peck, describes the consequences of making choices against health and openness.

Do whatever feels comfortable. If your parents can't or won't understand, your therapist can help you decide on the next best step. When we refuse to enable unhealthy practices, we become quite powerful. Therapy, Codependents Anonymous, and Al-Anon can help you discover how you've enabled your parents' unhealthiness and how to stop doing it. Refusing to enable old practices can have amazingly quick results.

If your parents can't take the steps toward the relationship you long to have with them, it will take time to get through this loss. It's a death really, the death of your hope for family. Sometimes we have to find family among those who aren't related by blood.

Perhaps your parent is still violating your boundaries—by asking inappropriate questions, by showing up uninvited, by triangulating with your partner, spouse, or children. You have the right to set the same limits with a thoughtless or intrusive parent that you'd set with a friend or a stranger.

You can refuse to answer a question. You can insist that your parent come to your house only when invited and refuse to let him in if he hasn't been invited. You can confront your spouse and your parent about triangulation.

If you're a parent and you've been leaning on your children, lean on someone else. Find a therapist you can depend on. Ask her to teach you how to become a good parent.

If your children have been very hurt, they may have quit trying. Approach them with your earnest desire to make amends for your mistakes so that you can build a new, healthy relationship. Several tough therapy sessions may be in store to heal past hurts.

Tina's Story

For years, I held the family together. My mother was very dependent on me and I felt responsible for whatever happened between us.
I made sure we had a relationship. When I first moved out she put
up no protest, but then I saw her start to fade. She wouldn't call
unless she was sad and needed to cry. Then whenever I went home,
she'd compete with my friends for my time. No matter how much
time I saved for her, it wasn't enough. She had all kinds of ways of
manipulating me to get me to choose her over my friends.

My mother used me as her main support. Whenever I brought up
something that was worrying me, in minutes she'd have the conversation turned around to an issue of hers. Years ago a boyfriend of
mine betrayed me but I already knew not to tell her about it. I'd
long since stopped trying. But she didn't see it. She'd still say to
me all the time, "You never talk to me about what's going on with
you."

The last time she said this—I'd been in therapy for a few years by
then and was losing my ability to cover things up—I didn't plan it,
but the words just popped out of my mouth. I said, "When I do try
to talk to you, you switch it to something about you. I start out
needing help and I end up helping you. I go away feeling emptier
than when I started."

"I don't do that," she said.

I didn't say anything. After a bit, she said, "Would you give me
another chance?"

I sat there not saying anything for about five minutes. Then I
said, "I'm really worried about Bob. I'm not sure I can trust him.
Since I've been here, he's been going to this place he only goes to
when he's looking for a woman."

Then my mother said—I couldn't believe it—she said, "How do
you think I feel? Your father used to go out on me all the time."
Then she started crying.

I said, "You just did it."

She stopped mid-tear. "You're right!" She was aghast. She finally
saw what she was doing.

Later I said I wasn't going to teach her how to communicate any
more or make sure we stayed in touch. She tried a few manipula-
tions, but I wasn't even tempted to fall for one. She said, "If you
don't teach me to communicate, who will?"

I said, "There are lots of people who would be glad to teach you, but it's not going to be me any more."

"What kind of people?"

"Therapists, people who give workshops. If you look, you'll find someone." She was still trying to guilt-trip me, but I didn't fall for any of it. I felt so strong and clear inside. I didn't have the rock in my stomach I used to get after a few minutes with her.

I left town and within four days she was in therapy. Within six months she was in treatment. Then she came to visit me and we spent five grueling hours in therapy together.

We have a wonderful relationship now. I have so much respect for her. She's gotten strong. She's taken charge of her life. She has better friendships. I'm amazed at her.

Wilma's Story

I'm Tina's mother. When my daughter confronted me, I didn't have any idea what she was talking about. I didn't realize I was leaning on her so much. I didn't realize I was letting her do all the work in our relationship.

When I first went to therapy, I had no idea what to expect. I didn't know what to say. It's like I had a hood over my eyes. There was so much to life I didn't know anything about. I didn't know about boundaries. I didn't realize Tina had been abused by her father.

It had never occurred to me that my incredible neediness made me neglect her. I was in the house but she grew up by herself.

This was very hard for me to hear. You can't imagine—the hardest thing I've ever done. But I could see that I would lose my daughter if I didn't learn to listen to her, and I'm at the point now where I can hear anything she has to say.

My therapist had to teach me how to be a mother. Sixty-five years old and learning to be a mother. Now when I call my daughter I ask what she's doing and how she's feeling. I listen without interrupting her and wait until she's entirely through before I talk about myself. Then I tell her things only for the purpose of sharing, not to get her to take care of me.

Last week I was asking Tina about her work and she said, "Mom, you're really getting the hang of this. This feels great!"

I didn't want to walk into my therapist's office the first time—in my day, that meant you were either crazy or weak; we didn't take our problems to strangers—but if I hadn't done that, if Tina hadn't had the courage to be the first one to do it, I might have lost my daughter. I might have spent the rest of my life wondering "Where is my daughter who I once treasured?"

CHAPTER TEN

A SPECIAL LETTER TO OVEREATERS

Food and Fat Seem to Protect Us

In *Anatomy of a Food Addiction,* my book for overeaters and food addicts, I revealed that I struggled for years with overeating and overweight. Then as the fat began to leave my body, I was astounded at how vulnerable and defenseless I felt.

If you are carrying extra weight, it may be providing you with a boundary as well. Weight is a good way to keep people at a distance when people have taken too much from you. It literally extends your physical boundary.

If you were abused as a child, fat can feel like a comforting shield. It is a physical barricade against people who might harm you.

Food and fat seem to protect us. Perhaps you eat more when you feel threatened. Perhaps you eat when you know someone is going to try to take more from you than you want to give. Perhaps you eat when you're with a person who assaults your boundaries.

Boundary development is an important companion to an eating recovery program. Not until you know you can protect yourself from intrusion and theft will you be safe without the extra weight.

Diets are a waste of time, sabotage is certain, if you need extra weight for safety or if food is the way you comfort yourself. Instead of setting yourself up for another failure, give yourself the opportunity to learn to meet your needs and protect yourself.

Weight, of course, is a complicated problem. Many people hope that when they do learn to protect themselves, the weight will melt automatically. But for most of us, other things need to be attended to. In any case, boundary formation is essential to recovering from bingeing. Attending to your insides is an important part of changing the outside.

Special Information for Compulsive or Addicted People

A compulsion or addiction keeps others at a distance. When you're lost in your drug, it's easy to shut out the demands of others. Shopping or running or working compulsively puts a nice canyon between you and your would-be intimates.

While you shut others out, you shut yourself in. Addictions and compulsions isolate you. They keep you from living and growing, from intimacy, and from confronting your issues and connecting with your life's purposes.

If you have children, the distance created by addictions and compulsions translates into neglect and abandonment. Believe it or not, too much distance can also be a boundary violation. If you are remote, who's loving your children?

Effective recovery includes developing healthy, clean boundaries. Good boundaries strengthen recovery and provide additional insurance against relapse. If you can give yourself the separateness you need when you need it, you'll decrease your dependence on a compulsion to do it for you. As your sobriety increases, you may discover you need distance. We advance our sobriety when we face our issues and challenge our fear of intimacy. Good boundaries allow us to be close to others without losing ourselves.

I encourage you to attend to your boundary development and to get whatever help you need to live a sober, conscious life.

CHAPTER ELEVEN

GOOD FENCES

Good Boundaries Yield Healthy Relationships

Best of luck building good boundaries. This process requires continued attention and maintenance. Someday, perhaps, most of us will understand boundaries and be sensitive to interactions that cross boundaries. But until that happy time, even well-meaning people will continue to intrude on personal territory.

Good boundaries enable us to define ourselves. They enhance our physical and emotional health and promote recovery. Good boundaries yield healthy relationships.

True intimacy is possible only between two whole, distinct people who both have good boundaries. Enmeshment feels like intimacy but it's not. How can you be intimate with someone who blends into you? Intimacy grows as you become known by the other and as you know the other. If the other person's individuality shifts and fades, how can you know this person? If your sense of yourself is wobbly, how can you be known?

As your boundaries get clearer, you'll reap riches. If you know what you want, you can get it. If you know yourself, you can get involved in what's important to you. The friends who respect your limits are the friendships that will be strengthened. True intimacy with a special person becomes possible.

The poet was right. Good fences do make good neighbors.

APPENDIX

SHARE YOUR EXPERIENCES WITH BOUNDARIES

The awareness of boundaries is relatively new, partially an outgrowth of creative developments in process psychology and context therapy, and partially a harvest from the growing population of recovering people. Mistakes, trial and error, and negative consequences from boundary errors have also contributed to the understanding that there are limits to what's appropriate within certain contexts.

You can contribute to the growing body of information by sharing your own experience with boundaries. Write about an incident involving boundaries and send it to me. The incident could be one in which you discovered a boundary for yourself; it could be about a relationship where the roles are confused and the boundaries are muddy; it could be one in which you suspect a boundary violation. Describe the situation as fully as possible.

Send your story to:

Anne Katherine
Parkside Publishing Corporation
205 West Touhy Avenue
Park Ridge, Illinois 60068-5881